New Guinea

In flight from Mount Hagen to Angoram in the Western Highlands district over one of the many tributaries of the Sepik River.

THIS BEAUTIFUL WORLD VOL. 34

New Guinea

by MILTON AND JOAN MANN

講談社

Published by
KODANSHA INTERNATIONAL LTD.
Tokyo, Japan & Palo Alto, Calif., U.S.A.

Distributed in Continental Europe by Boxerbooks, Inc., Zurich; in Canada by Fitzhenry & Whiteside Limited, Ontario; and in the Far East by Japan Publications Trading Co., P.O. Box 5030 Tokyo International, Tokyo. Published by Kodansha International Ltd., 2–12–21 Otowa, Bunkyo-ku, Tokyo 112, Japan, and Kodansha International/USA, Ltd., 599 College Avenue, Palo Alto, California 94306. *Printed in Japan.*

LCC 76–184666
ISBN 0–87011–166–3
JBC 0325–783301–2361

First edition, 1972

Contents

Acknowledgements

Mr. Lisle Newby of the Territorial Administration of Papua and New Guinea

Mr. Bryan T. Hill of the Papua and New Guinea Tourist Board

Mr. Brian Grey of Ansett Airlines of Papua New Guinea

Mr. David McEwan of Air Pacific

Encounter with New Guinea

People are what make a country interesting, and New Guinea has more than its fair share of interesting people. Approximately 2.3 million call it home. Organized simply, they fall into two categories: black and white. Whites have only been around on a permanent basis for the last eighty years. The majority are expatriots from Australia, Europe, and China.

Regardless of the fact that there are an ample number of shapely bodies running around, New Guinea is not for women! There are always those few who can overcome lack of conveniences and the niceties of life, or can live in small, closely knit communities without succumbing to the cattiness, infidelity, and eventual hate that stems from boredom. But the majority cannot. Eventually life is reduced to the numbers game as they count the days until their husbands' contracts with the administration lapse and they can return home. With a host of blood sucking pests, tropical diseases, unpredictable natives, miles of virgin bush, and the necessity of possessing a Rube Goldberg mind continually in high gear, the only conclusion possible is that New Guinea is for men.

On that point, both black and white agree. For in his country, the indigenous male (the somewhat unpleasant expatriot term for native men) is king. In his world, survival is the struggle. He demands respect not on a basis of good works but rather for courage and cunning. How well he survives the rituals of manhood initiation, wars with neighbors, and amasses fortunes with which to purchase wives, pigs, and other signs of his wealth are all part of his game of life. But his life-style of supremacy is disintegrating before the overflow of progress now creeping across his country. Up to half a dozen wives can still be bought as long as he can afford them. However, many women are no longer content with sticking around the home and tending their gardens. They are demanding jobs in town, and some insist on keeping the money they earn.

Though this may be true sociologically, political and economic prospects are bright. Administration police patrols moving on foot through the formidable country have brought a new civilization to the scantily clothed primitives. Under Australian supervision, intertribal wars have been brought pretty well under control. Whereas few previously ventured beyond their villages in fear of enemy reprisals, peace has brought new-found freedom to travel with little restraint. The flow and mingling of people has given many a better understanding of others. Tribal intermarriage is becoming common, making New Guinea's once fairly distinguishable races a hodgepodge. Colors vary from light tan to jet blue black.

Three primary groups inhabit the country. Melanesians populate the coastal regions and island areas. Papuans make up the bulk of the mainland, while some Negritoes are found near Madang. No one is sure of their origin except to generalize that they probably came from somewhere in Asia and possibly Indonesia. Smatterings of the other two major Pacific island peoples, Micronesians and Polynesians, are also found on the fringe islands.

Most of the people are concentrated in the Highlands, where it is cooler and relatively mosquito free. Similar to all Pacific island people, they are strongly attached to their land, but its ownership is vested in kinship groups as opposed to individuals. Everyone tends to live in small groups or clans numbering from twenty to three hundred. Hereditary chiefs are nonexistent. Leaders are elected solely on the basis of achievement and wealth, and buying an office is frequent. Lavish feasts and gift giving are used to gain prestige and, thereby, votes.

There is little suggestion of national unity. Competition between highland and coastal tribes is keen, and many fear independence from Australia because of this. The administration currently rules with a tight hand, but some native leaders feel that when independence comes they could again lose power to neighboring tribes who were bitter enemies a short time ago. In an effort to overcome this anxiety, the administration has been slowly teaching the forms of democracy. Their program was much accelerated shortly after World War II, when world opinion demanded eventual independence for New Guinea. Since 1964, the population has been electing a Government House of Assembly to help design rules for the country. Sixty-eight members have found politics a difficult and arduous task mainly because more than half the population still favors tradition over progress, while outside forces are demanding that a twentieth century B.C. New Guinea transform overnight into the twentieth century of today.

Education is crucial if this transformation is to be achieved. As money becomes available, the administration is taking over more of the responsibility of educating. However, the bulk of the job remains in missionary hands. The quality of instruction is the best they can do under difficult circumstances and with limited funds. Overall, it consists of little more than teaching the rudiments of reading and math and within a few years returning the majority of students to their villages. Confused and undereducated, many are too smart to be satisfied with village life and not highly enough trained for skilled jobs. For the few fortunate enough to succeed in finding a place, there are missionary run colleges equivalent to a high-school education in the United States. Trade schools and schools of medicine, dentistry, nursing, teaching, and crafts are being built as rapidly as possible. The University of Papua New Guinea in Port Moresby is the ultimate goal.

However, the main difficulty in educating the masses is not entirely the fault of lack of funds or improper priorities. Over seven hundred languages are spoken in the country; some used by as few as three hundred people. They are not just dialects but distinct, separate languages, which often vary from village to village. Currently the *lingua franca* of New Guinea is Melanesian Pidgin, which is understood by approximately thirty-seven percent of the population. Two others vie for honors as the national spoken language: Police Motu, devised from Papuan tongues by roving patrols years ago, is principally used in the south; English brought in by the administration is the third. The latter is taught in an increasing number of the schools.

In every man's *meri's* ("woman") and *pikinini's* ("child") search for a *wantok* (one who speaks the same language), though, it appears that Pidgin will win. Linguists insist it has merits and should be considered, particularly since a large number of people already speak it. For anyone interested in trying to learn this comparatively simple yet very colorful language, it is wisest to rely on books, several of which have been written on the subject. All express the idea that Pidgin is basically Melanesian and English with a touch of Malay, Chinese, and German. It has a rather limited vocabulary of a little over thirteen hundred words, yet it is possible to translate many thousands of English words into Pidgin.

Many expatriots consider it a form of baby talk and are careless in learning to speak the language, frequently causing problems of misunderstanding to arise between them and their indigenous employees. In fun, expatriots sometimes conjure up their own idioms. An often-heard phrase is "mixmaster belong Jesus Christ," supposedly meaning a helicopter. Undoubtedly only an extremely small number of indigenous have any idea of what an electric egg beater is. But they probably shrug off the statement and laughingly think to themselves what is perhaps the most useful word in Pidgin, *bagarapim* (pronounced bugerupem), which refers to any person or object not in a fit condition.

For those interested in semantics, New Guinea is not really New Guinea. The world's second largest island is actually divided into three portions, each bearing a different title. The entire western half is under Indonesian control and called West Irian. Prior to 1953 it was Dutch New Guinea, but in that year, United Nations and United States influence virtually forced the Dutch to leave. Very little is known about the development of the area since then. To outsiders it appears to have returned to its former wild state and remains the home of headhunters, cannibals, missionaries, occasional anthropologists, and an unstated number of Indonesian soldiers.

The eastern half is properly called the Territory of Papua and New Guinea. This title covers both the United Nations Trust Territory of New Guinea to the north and the Australian owned possession of Papua to the south. Since 1946, an agreement with the United Nations has given Australia the right to administer both portions and prepare them for eventual independence. This book is solely concerned with the Territory of Papua and New Guinea (hereafter referred to as TPNG or the Territory).

TPNG is located in the South Pacific Ocean at 1° to 12° latitude south of the equator and 141° to 160° east longitude. One hundred miles of water in the Torres Straits separate it from Queensland, Australia. Land area totals three hundred four thousand square miles. This includes not only the main island but some six hundred outer islands and archipelagoes. Trobriand, Woodlark, and D'Entrecasteaux islands plus the Louisiade Archipelago are part of Papua. The Bismarck Archipelago, which includes the Admiralty Islands, New Ireland and New Britain, and the northern Solomon Islands of Bougainville and Buka, forms part of the Territory of New Guinea.

Weather is generally tropical. Northwest monsoons begin in December and continue through March; Southwest monsoons, from May through October. Rainfall varies erratically from valley to valley. In some places it can be as little as sixty inches while elsewhere as much as three hundred inches per year. Temperatures hover between seventy-five and eighty-six degrees Fahrenheit. However, because the relative humidity is generally above seventy-five percent, it feels hot and sticky most of the time. Coastal regions are the least comfortable. Yet in the Highlands it is pleasant by day, with nights cool enough to require blankets for sleeping.

Botanically the Territory is considered part of the Indo-Malayan region. However, the flora has much in common with northern Australia. Except in low rainfall areas, most of the country is covered with luxuriant rain forests. There are no deserts or extremely arid zones. Mountain areas rise from alpine forests to tundra where snow falls on occasional peaks. A profusion of exotic flowers, including a wide variety of orchids, grow wild. Spotted croton leaves add to the color. Although a variety of trees cover the landscape, palms, growing up to an altitude of fifteen hundred feet, are the most useful. Sago, coconut and Areca, or betel nut, palms are popular sources of food and shelter.

For all its prolific growth in flora one would expect fauna to be equally abundant, but this is not the case. Fleshy meat is scarce, and most people rely on vegetables for sustenance. Fauna is also akin to Australia in that over one hundred marsupials predominate. Cuscus and the red bandicoot are prevalent, with the wallaby or tree kangaroo the largest in size. Lizards, tortoises, and crocodiles favor the rivers and tidal swamps, while more than seventy species of snake, including pythons, haunt the rest of the country. Among the pests, leeches prefer the rain forests, May- and sandflies inhabit the beaches, while mosquitoes seem to be everywhere. Of the plentiful birds, only the cassowary and numerous species of bird of paradise are of native origin. Parrots, cockatoos, and others were imported at one time or another from Australia and Malaysia.

Portugese explorers were credited with being the first Europeans to arrive in New Guinea during the sixteenth century. Antonio d'Abreu and Francesco Serram reported examining the north coast but failed to name it. In 1526 the Portugese Don Jorge de Meneses named the country *Illpas dos Papuas* from the Malay word meaning land of frizzy-haired people. Ynigo Ortis de Retez of Spain sailed the north coast in 1545. Believing that the people resembled those of African Guinea, he named the island New Guinea.

The seventeenth century brought the Dutch, and the eighteenth, the British. It was not until 1824 that The Netherlands and Britain signed a treaty acknowledging the Dutch claim over the west half of the island. Four years later the Dutch formally annexed the area.

With Dutch interest increasing, Australians in nearby Queensland became worried about foreign domination coming too close to home. They demanded that the British take over the eastern half of New Guinea, but things remained stagnant for the next twenty-five years. It was not until 1884, when the Germans moved in and claimed the north coast and the Bismarck Archipelago, that the British became worried and finally claimed a protectorate over the southeast coast.

Australia formally came into the picture in 1906, when the British gave them control of Papua. World War I saw the Australians invade German New Guinea and assume a military government over the area for the next seven years. Under a mandate of the League of Nations, Australia assumed civil administration of German New Guinea in 1921, and the country remained politically stable until the Japanese invaded. After three centuries of successive foreign rule, since World War II TPNG has rapidly advanced towards its ultimate goal of independence.

Modern-day visitors will find New Guinea considerably changed from the land the explorers of the sixteenth century discovered. The once impenetrable interior now contains 360 airports and over nine thousand miles of roads. After an entry permit has been issued by the Department of External Territories, Canberra, Australia, in behalf of the administrator of TPNG, all one needs is a smallpox vaccination, a bottle of antimalaria pills, and a pair of shorts and matching long socks, and one is prepared for New Guinea.

ENCOUNTER WITH NEW GUINEA

Port Moresby

Five minutes after disembarking at Port Moresby's Jackson's Airport it became apparent that the price of adventure was going to be high! If we intended to see New Guinea on a shoestring, it had better be laced through a combat boot. The girl at the airport information counter was quite disturbed over the fact that we did not have hotel reservations. It was Christmas and many people were in town for the holidays. Not wishing to delay our trip, we decided to take whatever was available and skip dinner that night to balance our budget. The Davara Hotel certainly appeared out of context. It had a swimming pool, was air conditioned, and the dining room required guests dress for dinner. The only hint of the primitive New Guinea we had read so much about decorated the walls in the form of carvings.

Captain John Moresby, Royal Navy, discovered the site of Port Moresby in 1873. One year later, the London Missionary Society established a small colony. When the Japanese were driven out at the end of World War II, the total population stood at three thousand. Today, the figure has reached fifty-six thousand (forty-two thousand five hundred indigenous; thirteen thousand five hundred Europeans), and, still growing, it is the town with the largest population in the Territory. Its layout resembles a creeping vine whose roots are firmly embedded on the ocean's edge. For seven miles in three directions the feelers crawl into the surrounding hillsides. Of the multitude of suburbs, Boroko is the fastest growing. A modern shopping center, theater, hotel, and several restaurants cover its landscape. Boroko is one of the few areas where Chinese stores are well interspersed with European shops.

Moresby's overall appearance is that of a resort town. It is divided in half by one major roadway, which becomes clogged with traffic only at noon and five in the afternoon. At those hours a policeman stands beneath the inaccurate clock in the center of town and waves his arms rather hysterically in an effort to straighten out the mess. His job is easy, for within ten minutes the exodus does it for him, and normal peace and quiet resume.

Any place downtown is within easy walking distance. Burns Philp and Steamships Trading Company provide the population with dry goods. Each features well-stocked supermarkets whose shelves bulge with food from Australia, New Zealand, and England. Most meat and dairy products are frozen. Prices, considering the usually exorbitant cost of island living, are rather reasonable. The rest of the town consists of a scattering of miscellaneous stores catering to local needs, a couple of banks, souvenir shops, book, watch, and camera dealers, and airline offices. An office building of eleven stories is the only skyscraper in the country. Other buildings average two floors. Port area wharves complete the picture.

After one night of comparative luxury, our second day in New Guinea was spent in the quest of a cheaper hotel. We located a Hungarian named Harrison who ran a guest house. Harrison's biggest drawback was being located six miles from town. There were buses but no apparent schedules. We made several attempts to ride them but discovered hitchhiking was faster and more reliable. Along with the rides came several verbal attempts to initiate us into the glories of the Territory. The ride of six miles rather limited conversations to a few exchanges of pleasantries, generally two points of interest and a lot of criticism. Koki Market, gathering place of the indigenous, and the swimming beach in the heart of downtown were the points of interest. And "Moresby is filled with misfit expatriots and disgruntled indigenous" was the gist of the criticism.

We spent a week in Moresby laying plans for our forthcoming photographic efforts. We have always found government cooperation helpful in producing educational films, and Mr. Lisle Newby of the Department of Information and Extension Services was precise, knowledgable, and unusually understanding of our requirements. We also paid a visit to the Tourist Board. Bryan T. Hill, its director, was a flamboyant and trifle eccentric genius who initiated imaginative ideas for promoting tourism. His current pride was an educational booklet he had just produced. Entitled *Bisnis Bolong Turis*, it was a clever pamphlet written entirely in Pidgin explaining the concept and benefits of tourism to the natives. Mr. Hill was pleased to have another opportunity to show off New Guinea.

Transportation arrangements were made through Ansett Airlines of Papua New Guinea. Ansett also provided us with brochures advertising hotels in the Territory's major towns. Both transportation and accommodations were quite expensive. But the airlines had good cause. Unpredictable weather, rugged mountainous terrain, poor communications, high salaried expatriot crews, extensive maintenance, rough landing strips, and long distances to alternate airports are all factors that add to the conventional costs of operating a domestic airline. Flying over New Guinea is serious business. We felt that our personal safety was well worth the expense, so we made a final check of our equipment and headed for Jackson's Airport.

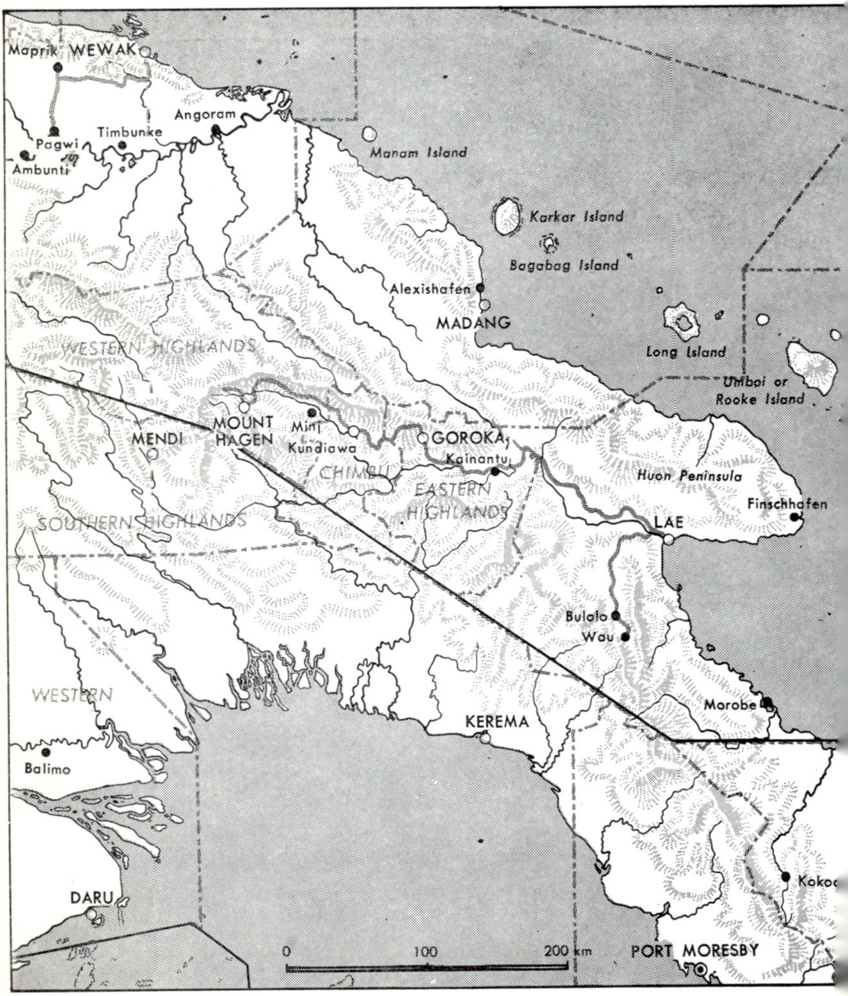
Maprik
WEWAK
Angoram
Timbunke
Pagwi
Ambunti
Manam Island
Karkar Island
Bagabag Island
Alexishafen
MADANG
Long Island
Umboi or
Rooke Island
WESTERN HIGHLANDS
MOUNT
HAGEN
Mini
Kundiawa
MENDI
GOROKA
Kainantu
CHIMBU
EASTERN
HIGHLANDS
Huon Peninsula
Finschhafen
LAE
SOUTHERN HIGHLANDS
Bulolo
Wau
WESTERN
Morobe
KEREMA
Balimo
DARU
0
100
200 km
PORT MORESBY

On and Off the Beaten Track

Lae

Lae is the industrial capital of the Territory. Three hundred fifty miles of highway make it the only seaport town in New Guinea with driveable access to the interior. It is the home of South Pacific Brewery, and the proud possessor of the only eighteen-hole golf course in the country.

When gold was discovered in the Morobe District in the late 1920s, a supply base was needed to transport equipment to the gold fields. Lae, then a tiny village, was chosen. The reason was not spectacular. Lae happened to have the largest piece of flat land available for building an airport. Disassembled gold dredges were air freighted via modified Junker aircraft to the nearby mines of Bulolo.

When the gold petered out, the mining companies looked around for more. They did not find it. Realizing all that's gold does not glitter, they turned their attention to the verdant tropical forest. Today, Bulolo is home to one of the largest and most modern plywood factories in the world. Australia and the United States are the prime recipients of the thirty-five million square feet of the 3/16-inch product that the mill produces annually. Japanese companies are also making bids for a share of New Guinea's timber.

Lae is built around that airstrip, which now serves the entire Territory. The town center, only one-half mile away, sits on a bluff overlooking the field. Downtown is shared by an almost equal number of stores and government buildings. It is a sleepy, beautiful place.

The Chinese community is one mile from the airport on the valley floor. Their local business district rings a small village green. Stores were practically on top of each other. Despite their overwhelming number and close proximity, all appeared to have their fair share of business. Doorways and interiors were crowded with people licking ice cream and sipping soft drinks. Goods were crammed everywhere possible, from glass enclosed counters to the rafters above. A few things were imported from Hong Kong and Taiwan, while the majority came from mainland China. Nothing had the appearance of quality.

Seeto and Sons were apparently the most prolific family. Signs bearing that title appeared on the majority of buildings. We struck up a conversation with one of the Mr. Seetos, although his English was not too good. We inquired if he had recently immigrated from China. "My family come three generations past. We built Chinese schools. Now my children go to government schools. Speak good English." While discussing things Chinese, he invited us to see his gardens in the rear of the store. Many vegetables were growing on fish ponds. But his pride and joy was a new, nearly completed swimming pool. He doubted it would ever be finished. "Everybody talk independence. Before it come, we go south (Australia). Already have airplane tickets for whole family."

The Botanical Gardens provided comic relief for us after a brief visit to the city's famous war cemetery. Nowhere else have we seen botanical gardens where people picked the flowers. Fortunately, the indigenous preferred to decorate their hair with the common hibiscus flowers and croton leaves and left the exotic orchids to their pots.

The trees in the gardens drew our thoughts to the original reason we came to Lae. Lumber is one key to New Guinea's future economic independence. We needed photos to explain that point in our educational film. The government is doing everything possible to promote the lumber industry. Reforestation, a school of forestry, and experimental tree farms are all part of the plan. However, as it turned out we never saw Bulolo's plywood factory. Heavy rains flooded the road from Lae. Instead, three forestry men took us to Oomsis experimental nursery.

Afterwards we stopped at a village. Western influence was evident especially in the housing. Poorly constructed buildings dotted the community. Children were swimming in a nearby stream. Frightened women watched us from darkened doorways. Only a few men moved about, save for one woman engrossed in weaving a *bilum* bag, who ignored our approach.

Bilums are the carryalls of the indigenous. They are similar to shopping bags in shape but attain the size of roughly four by four feet. Reed grasses are used as the basic weaving material. A long band similar to a handle is attached to the opening. This band is worn across the forehead, while the bag is left to dangle loose on the back. Although *bilums* hold a variety of goods, the favorite items usually include bottles, bananas, and babies, with the latter frequently sandwiched between the others.

Lumber was largely an export industry. We also wanted to see a product intended solely for local consumption. South Pacific

Brewery appeared the logical choice. Drinking seemed the national pastime. The German-born brewmaster was pleased to show us his operation. Beer making is an art fraught with complications; running a plant in a remote country only made things more difficult. At least he had the expert advice of Heineken brewery in Europe, which provided technical assistance whenever possible.

One of the biggest headaches was trying to keep the brewery building cool in the tropics. Copper cookers can raise the temperature to unbearable levels. A simple styrofoam roof supported by steel beams and surrounded by wire mesh walls provided the answer: the location of South Pacific Brewery along the ocean allowed full advantage to be taken of nature's own air conditioning—sea breezes blowing through the open structure.

Bottles were another problem. Import costs were high, since they had to come from either Australia or Japan. Australian Consolidated Industries decided to create a local bottle factory, which would not only help alleviate the flow of currency leaving the country for bottles but also provide jobs for the indigenous. It was a good scheme and will probably be better once their inexperienced crews improve the forty percent breakage they currently suffer.

New Guinea's soda pop bottlers are also anxious to have the bottle plant operating at full capacity. Ten-cent bottles of "lolly water" are the best drinks New Guineans on limited budgets can afford. For that reason lolly water manufacturing is a large business. It would not remain low cost, however, if bottlers had to pay air transport costs to distribute their products throughout the country. So each district center has its own bottlers, and most distribution is limited to the distance that roads run into the bush.

Unlike beer, lolly water is rebottled in the same container. Yet because so much is consumed in remote villages, many bottles are never returned. They represent a high cost to the bottler. In order to reduce their costs, most lolly water bottlers have taken to buying all the used South Pacific beer bottles they can obtain. This has created a profitable business for some people. Women in particular roam the streets collecting every bottle they find lying around. Garbage men pick them out of trash cans. Pubs and hotels sort them from other refuse into separate bins, and even the prison chain gangs cutting grass along the highways pick up those they find in the bush. Anyone willing to bring them to a bottler is paid cash. Some women make as much as eighty dollars a month, which is a good income in the Territory. Hotels and garbage men are happy for the extra profits, and the prisoners earn while they pay. "The only one who doesn't benefit is us," lamented the brewmaster. Nevertheless, his business seemed to be flourishing.

We were good friends with the brewmaster by the time the interview had come to a close. "Goroka is our next destination," we said. "You're going by the Highlands Highway, of course," he replied. Many had recommended the highway as the only way to really see the Highlands. He agreed. "You must not fly," he continued. "Highland Motors is taking a load of beer to Goroka tomorrow morning. The manager is my good friend. If you don't mind riding in the cab of a truck, I'm sure he'll let you go along."

Highlands Highway

Our first breakdown occurred before we even got on the road. We had been scheduled to ride in the air-conditioned cab of a U.S. manufactured White truck. White vehicles were reputed to be the finest, provided the road was paved. The Highlands Highway was not. Dust from the road frequently clogged the air brake filtering system of the trucks, causing the brakes to lock. Highland Motors owned several White vehicles, but all of them were out of order that day.

When we arrived at the terminal, the last of the cargo was being loaded on a Japanese Isuzu truck. However, three hours elapsed before we left. Most of that time was spent covering the cargo with insurance against highway robbery. Local villagers like to wait in the bush along steep grades. As a truck struggles up the difficult climb, men boost themselves onto its rear. Goods are unloaded to friends running below. By the time the truck reaches the crest of a hill, it has been relieved of its cargo. Covering freight with large tarpaulins tied down with nylon cables was the present solution. Completely enclosed bodies appeared to be the next step.

We studied the front bumper. A massive steel concoction resembling a steam engine's cowcatcher covered not only the grill but protruded on all sides. The manager explained that we would see many similarly equipped vehicles on the highway. Odds were favorable that we would be clipped on the narrow road. The bumper prevented damage to the truck.

Road building in New Guinea is best described as the scheme of a lunatic. One can hardly blame a madman, however. The fault lies entirely with New Guinea. Its rugged terrain can never be aptly described. In profound understatement, one patrol officer explained how frustrating it was. "Early in the morning, I shouted across to the village on the next ridge that I was on my way. Late that evening I reached my destination completely exhausted. As the crow flies the distance was less than a mile." Frequent rains either wash sections of the road away or make it so muddy that only a skier would be able to maneuver through the slick mud. Landslides constantly block passage. Yet for all its faults, our driver John praised it continually as the best road in the Territory.

The first one hundred miles of driving were comparatively easy. Lazily the road wound through the floor of the Markham Valley. Only a few Bailey bridges spanned the Markham River and its tributaries. They could easily be replaced when washed away, as always happens during the rainy season. Cattle grazing was the predominant form of agriculture. Most land was covered with kuni grass, a tough, unmanageable weed that prospered. Entire mountains were covered with it. Slash and burn techniques of farming left the earth too poor to support anything else.

About midpoint we stopped for lunch at a local version of a truck stop. The menu was monotonous—cocount was the only dish offered. First we drank the juice, then ate the meat for food. Foothills came up suddenly. Within a matter of minutes we climbed five thousand feet into Kassam Pass. A turnoff near the crest allowed us to look back over the Markham Valley. Even in the twilight it had a majestic quality.

A monument close by was dedicated to a man who helped create the road through the pass. Back in 1953 he, several patrol officers, and a host of local villagers had cut a dry weather road across the treacherous slopes. An interesting fact pointed out in the administration's handbook *Districts of Papua New Guinea, 1969* stated: "Traffic over this 5,000 foot high road increased from 70 to 80 vehicles in the 1957 dry season, to six a day for nine months of 1962." Even today traffic is not exactly rush-hour density.

John became excited at Kainantu, a small town along the way.

"Here to Goroka, road is nambawan (number one)!" Dillingham Corporation was paid three million dollars to grade and straighten it. Our first thought was that Dillingham had been considerably overpaid. Then John showed us portions of the original road climbing straight up mountains and clinging to cliffs. Although we could not fully agree with John as to the highway's superiority, it did have improvements we would see nowhere else in New Guinea: drainage ditches along the shoulders to catch runoff rain, gentle, well-banked turns wherever possible, and reflective guard posts marking dangerous curves. It was the safest road in New Guinea, and a landmark in road building history.

A few days later, when we felt our saddle sores had healed, we looked for transportation to Mount Hagen. The road between the two towns was so rough that even Avis refused to try harder and would not rent cars to drive the distance. We settled on a Talco Tour bus. Jim was our expatriot driver. He knew the area very well, having lived there for a number of years. Between explanations of passing scenery he discussed life among the Highlanders.

Unofficially he and his wife had adopted an indigenous girl. "We found her wandering though Kundiawa one afternoon covered with blisters. Her mother had become irate because the girl failed to tend her young brother properly. The woman threw her into a fire. Since no one appeared to care, we took her into our home. Now we'd like to adopt her officially, but the family is holding us up. She's thirteen, and the father knows in a couple more years she'll be worth a bride price."

Currently Jim's wife and "daughter" were on holiday in Australia. That created another problem. His daughter had lingered on Australian beaches too long and tanned to a deeper brown than usual. She protested returning to New Guinea for fear her people would consider her an outcast. Racial prejudice is rife among the indigenous. Bukas of the northern Solomon Islands are about the darkest people on earth. To be as "black as a Buka" is slanderous among the vast majority of rich chocolate brown-colored people of New Guinea.

We left Goroka late in the afternoon and passed little of interest before dark except people walking their pigs. Pigs are the most prized possession in the country and rank second only to men in status. Wherever they go, families take their pigs with them, tied to ropes like dogs. Jim was careful not to hit the animals. Pigs killed unceremoniously upset the tribes. Only large cash settlements satisfy their anger. Drivers who think they can hit and run do not have a chance. Natives figure that what passes by one way must eventually return. Groups of villagers band together and sit on the road waiting for the reappearance of the offender.

We might have made Hagen in one day if we had not left Goroka so late in the afternoon. Chimbu Lodge in Kundiawa was our overnight stop. It was a stroke of good luck that gave us the opportunity of seeing the Chimbu District by daylight. In area, Chimbu is the smallest district, covering only 2,260 square miles. Figures showed it has the largest population density with 180,000 indigenous and 345 expatriots. Topographically it is the loveliest region in New Guinea. Neat hillside gardens of sweet potatoes spill off the village-lined ridges like chocolate frosting dripped on a cake. Flowers bloom everywhere. It has the appearance of Switzerland in summer.

A crowd had gathered in the village of Kondo, and we pulled off the road to see what was happening. Village men were busy making *ounguns*, traditional bow-tie shaped drums. Methods used were primitive, but they resulted in a cultural achievement. Steel axes shaped the exteriors from lengths of round tree trunks. Interiors were hollowed out by dropping hot stones into their centers, which eventually burned completely through. Perforated tin cans nailed to sticks were used as sandpaper to smooth out the holes. Sound depends on the thickness of the wood and depth of the hole. The young men confessed they are not as proficient as their elders. Old men always know what sound will be produced before the drum is finished. Possum, snake, or lizard skins were fastened with tree gum on one end. Spots of the same gum were applied to the skins to produce different tones. Finished drums are rarely painted. Rather, they are stored in house rafters above the cooking fires until smoked black. This cures the wood and eliminates termites.

Within a few miles, Jim came to a screeching halt. In the bush moved a kaleidoscope of color. Beneath the plumage were bodies well slicked in pig grease and decorated with paint, beads, seeds, fur, and aluminum Christmas ornaments. Villagers were preparing for a singsing. Headdresses were spectacular masses of feathers. Reds, blues, and greens came from parrots, while cockatoos provided the white, and every other hue imaginable was once a bird of paradise. Highly prized bird feathers can cost as much as fifty dollars each. Together with pigs and shells they constitute the wealth of a man. However, headdresses may not be entirely the property of one man. Feathers, like other property, are kinship owned and often lent to make up a single creation. Because of their high value and to prevent extinction of the birds, it is illegal to sell feathers to Europeans for export purposes.

Translated, the gist of the sign we saw on a fence stated that all *wantoks* were invited to a party. Forty cents bought dinner, and sixty cents included beer. The village was holding a pig kill, and we had arrived at the most opportune time. Hunks of juicy pork were being pulled out from the mess of rocks and leaves constituting the underground oven. Naked women giggled as they pulled hot *kaukau* ("sweet potatoes") from a steaming fire. Behind them stood cases of South Pacific beer.

Apparently versed in the things that thrill tourists, the men laughingly held pig heads up for photos. Some posed chomping on pig's legs, while others pretended to eat *kaukau*. Everyone jostled to get into pictures. Then a young voice behind Milton asked politely if he would take a picture of an old man. Half-blind, the man patiently posed in the hot sun. Later the voice explained that the party was really in honor of this senior citizen. Everyone knew he was old and would die soon. It was traditional to have a party for him while he was still around to enjoy it.

Goroka

Goroka Public Market proved a good place to study local fashions. Our "best undressed" award went to the Bena Bena girls. They favored Indian type trade beads liberally strung in ropes and draped about their hips. Adornments of lacelike beaded collars around their necks completed their outfits. Perhaps it was the red, white, and blue colors that attracted our American eyes. Other styles of dress fluctuated from mini grass skirts to maxi loincloths. Heavy-duty leather belts occasionally beaded with the words "New Guinea" held most coverings in place. Whereas cloth preserved modesty, sheaths of leaves called by the Pidgin term "ass grass" appropriately concealed leftovers.

People willingly posed for photos, but most expected payment in return. Ten cents did not seem much, but the administration considers it a form of begging. Except for those few who make posing for pictures a full-time business, tipping is discouraged. Giving of cigarettes, candy or shells is the recommended alternative in an effort to keep picture taking on a friendly basis.

Every district of New Guinea has public markets usually, held on Wednesday and Saturday mornings. Farmers from the surrounding area bring in *bilums* full of goods. *Kaikai* ("food") includes sweet potatoes, pumpkins, squash, bananas, pineapples, peanuts, and betel nut. For Western atuned tastes, the Highland farmers grow carrots, tomatoes, onions, and green beans. There is no visible bargaining, because a sign at the market entrance states fixed rates for each item. Prices are set by the local council. Yet among the indigenous, an understanding exists. Everywhere in the world there is someone who can get it wholesale.

Intertribal warfare in New Guinea has diminished to a vast extent. But superstition still complicates matters. As one indigenous put it, "Before the missionaries came we used to believe in many devils. Now we don't believe in as many." Few people die from disease or natural causes. Such a disaster is believed caused by an enemy who has put a *puripuri* on his victim. *Puripuris* are similar to Caribbean island voodoo spells. Fear overtakes reason, and a man dies without visible cause. Modern medicine is helpless against the mind drenched in fear. Newspaper accounts continually tell of people who died due to mysterious circumstances. One man expired because a papaya fell from a tree onto his stomach. The fallen fruit caused his abdomen to swell. An enemy had obviously put a spell on him. If the person is lucky enough to discover stronger magic than that which his enemy possesses, the spell can be canceled. If not, he dies. It then becomes the job of his *wantoks* to avenge his death. Paybacks, as these vendettas are called, usually involve only a few people. However, shortly after our departure from the Highlands, about five thousand tribesmen went on a rampage. Luckily strangers are spared unless they happen to be wandering members of the enemy clan.

On the other hand, people of the Eastern Highlands District, of which Goroka is the headquarters, are among the most practical and realistic in the country. Eager for economic advancement, they have taken rapidly to new ideas. Local councils know that the value of dollars spent today will increase profits tomorrow. Some travel to other parts of the country not only for economic gain but because they are curious to see how others live. Those who prefer to remain may farm coffee, vegetables, or cattle. They rely on tourism to bring a bit of the world to them.

For tourists, Goroka's famous mudmen are the main attraction, and we took the Talco Tour to their village in the nearby Ascaro Valley. According to legend, the village of Makehuku was attacked by a neighboring tribe one day. During the battle several Makehuku men were murdered by the attackers. The rest of the villagers ran into the bush until the foray was over. In silence they watched as the enemy carried off their women and children. Revenge was planned for that same evening. While the victors were celebrating, the Makehuku men silently danced into their opponents' village. Covered in grayish river mud, they pretended to represent the spirits of the deceased victims. Clay masks with pig tusks, dog teeth, and features of shells completed the ghostly apparitions. Terrified, the recent conquerors fled into the bush, leaving the prisoners to be reunited with their clan. Makehuku Village was never attacked again.

The dance was relatively simple. Men silently stepped from the bush into the village waving leaves as they came. The overcast sky blended in well with the grass houses and added the proper atmosphere to accentuate the performance. It must have been a chilling sight to its original audience.

After the dance we had the opportunity to browse through the village. Homes of merry-go-round shapes were made from wood and grass. Interiors were pitch black except for small fires, which smoldered day and night. They were used for cooking and to take the chill off the cool evening air. The smoke also kept insects at bay, although at five thousand feet malarial mosquitoes are no problem.

By the light of our flash units we could see that their possessions were meager. It hardly seemed worth the effort of putting a padlock on the entrance. But every home bore a lock. Locks are unusual on Pacific islands. Communal living is normally prevalent, and possessions of others are free for the asking. In New Guinea, however, a key is a status symbol.

A crowd gathered in the bush. We went to see what was happening. A number of stakes and a distant target revealed an archery match about to commence. Ten cents per arrow was the fee. Silver coins glistened in the palm of one of the village men. The sight of the tour group made some of the archers set their aim for a little profit. Instead of shooting the arrows, they tried to sell them to the tourists. Arrows averaged four feet in length. Bamboo shafts bore tips that varied according to the prey desired. Five-pronged notched arrows were for birds; metal prongs for fish; and one giant-sized arrow was presumably for larger game. Its prongs were tied loosely with cane, which untied on impact, causing the arrow to spring open within the wound. For men and the target they used standard straight arrows with notched tips carved of black palm hardwood.

Near the archery course stood an old man clutching a fist of well-used arrows. He watched the selling action but did not join the bargaining. One of the arrows in his bunch struck my eye as being very old and particularly well carved. He appeared puzzled at my request to buy it but readily agreed. To him it was just a well-used arrow, but to me a genuine remembrance of New Guinea.

Mount Hagen

Mount Hagen was billed as the place where civilization has come closest to the Stone Age. Only thirty-five years old, it is one of the youngest district centers and appeared to be prospering. It held more shops and stores than Goroka, but the surrounding area looked barren. The Western Highlands were not as lush as the Eastern Highlands or Chimbu districts.

Agriculturally it was a success. Coffee was the principal crop. Tea was being tested as an alternative. Prospects for the latter product appeared good. Agricultural officials believe it may achieve internationally outstanding quality. Large grazing areas made cattle ranching popular. Sheep had been tried but the herds were decimated by bacteria and disease. Passion fruit and pyrethrum grew well and warranted the establishment of processing plants for each product. Cottee's used the passion fruit to produce their popular Passionatta soft drink. Pyrethrum, the daisylike plant used in insecticides, was having a little more difficulty. The plant took more work to cultivate and harvest, and the indigenous preferred the easier cash crop of coffee.

People of the Hagen area looked more African in dress and features. Frizzy hair, so prevalent on other New Guineans, turned woolly. It was worn in tassels emanating from the top of the head. Cloaks of vivid colors were wrapped about bodies in a style similar to that of the Masai of Kenya and Tanzania. Leather belts were replaced with foot-wide carved bands of wood bark. They appeared to have been hollowed from a solid chunk of tree. The puzzle was how they put them on. Loincloths were hung over the fronts, while ass grass covered rears.

We went to a pig kill one afternoon in the company of an indigenous government guide. By the time we arrived the festivities were over. Doggie bags of massive hunks of pork were being carted home, but a few of the participants remained. The feast was attended by some of the most strangely dressed men. If older generations of America think they have hairy problems, they ought to go to New Guinea and see the antics of its younger generation. Waghi Valley people favored wigs in the shape of Captain Bligh hats. Women and children contributed their clipped curls to form the creations. How the superstructures were held together was something only their hairdressers knew. Adornment was limited to a few leaves or cigarette package labels. Other men of the Western Highlands wore hairnets woven of material similar to *bilums*. Tufts of cuscus fur were intertwined to give the mesh a fuzzy semblance. Nets enclosed their own hair and shaped it into bulbous proportions. It gave the appearance of a confined Afro-American cut held in place with bones and feathers. Tattoos and body painting were nonexistent. Pig-greased bodies covered with clipped hair were the vogue.

It was difficult to tell the age of anyone. Those who appeared sixty were probably forty. Low protein diet and continual exposure to the elements made their skin shrivel. Wrinkles hung like drapes, and women's breasts were reduced to mere flaps of skin. No one was fat. Where skin retained its smoothness, muscles protruded.

Not caring to repeat the feat and go back down the highway, the only way left was up, which meant a TAL flight to Angoram on the Sepik River. Fearless was the best description of the TAL pilot of our plane. Freight schedules have to be kept, so once in a while a bush pilot will take a chance and illegally fly straight through clouds. Lack of radar on their small planes fails to inform them that a mountain stands between them and their destination. In rare instances some have lost their lives. "Most of the time I only carry freight," our pilot explained as we took off. "Sacks of produce, spare machine parts, or wriggling bags of livestock. Some times the dead body of a murdered man has to be brought into the government station so the *kiaps* [Pidgin for any government official] can investigate the killing. Lots of routine and boring stuff."

Money surely could not be their only compensation. We studied the passing landscape below. Flying from the Western Highlands to the Sepik River was similar to watching an exhibition of breathtaking jewels. Faceted emerald green mountains were set in ribbons of muddy rivers. In between the trees, as tight looking as the frizzy hair of the Papuans, sun-struck pools of water glistened in the Sepik swamplands.

Angoram

It is only natural, after globetrotting hundreds of thousands of miles, for friends to continually remark that we have been to the ends of the earth. We only smile. Then we discovered Angoram. There is no way to describe Angoram except from the beginning.

A blast of heat enveloped us as we opened the doors of the airplane. It was Saturday noon. Temperature and humidity formed a mutual agreement and had equalized themselves at ninety. The contents of our plane were met by a former-school-teacher-hotel-manager-tour-operator and droves of mosquitoes. The ratio was one man to the five of us and perhaps a dozen mosquito bites each.

The lone member of our welcoming party assumed the guise of tour operator and informed us that the hotel was "over there," a destination not clearly designated by his flailing hands. He then marched off in that general direction. Lack of porters was the gentle hint that all of us had better carry our own luggage lest it become moldy on the grass airstrip. Behind a row of bushes was a dirt road. Behind another row of bushes a quarter mile later was the hotel.

The tour-operator-turned-hotel-manager kindly offered us the use of his car to see Angoram. We thanked him but returned it fifteen minutes later. Angoram's highways consisted of two short gravel roads. One ran circles around the airport and village green and a short distance into the bush. A few houses, the hotel, four trade stores, and the only visible church dotted its byways. The second, rather appropriately named Tobacco Road, ran along the Sepik. Riverfront property included more homes, a lumber mill, a few more trade stores, and the boat landing. Surrounding suburbs were low-cost grass housing.

Trade stores were the principal tourist sights. Shelves were somewhat barren and offered little variety. About the only thing in ample quantity was beer, sometimes cold, and lolly water in three assorted flavors. Bartering is no longer the principal means of exchanging goods. Angoram's stores favor cash. Natives often try their hand at running trade stores. They soon go out of business, Europeans laughingly told us: "They are terrible businessmen. Have no sense of value. End up giving their stock away and are forced to close shop." One trader was not so sure they were foolish. "They're a communal society, everything share and share alike. Whoever has the goods is expected to give them away. However, it puts a debt on the recipient. After closing his store, the former trader probably retires for life living off the people obligated to support him."

We returned to the hotel and inquired what else was doing. The busy bartender looked up and said "cricket." We are glad to report the weekly Angoram match between indigenous and expatriots was in the best British tradition of keeping one's eyes on the ball—and nothing else. A large brush fire loomed behind the playing field. Everyone ignored the rapidly spreading holocaust even when ashes began falling like black snow and the heat became unbearable. Not until the fire began chewing away the perimeter of the playing field did the Assistant District Commissioner look up from his position and decide that something should be done.

The order was given. Prisoners from the local calaboose were released. To show their status in society, members of this unvolunteer fire brigade were replete in striped, traditional Pacific island skirts of cloth called "lavalavas." Within minutes after their arrival, the flames were subdued. By the time our eyes reverted back to the game, we realized that the only reason the ADC had looked up was because the match was over. However, the time we spent watching the event had been fruitful. We had met Rudy Treutlein.

1. *Specially designed aircraft,* such as ▶ this Twin Otter, are used to provide scheduled transportation into otherwise inaccessible parts of the country.

NEW GUINEA

Rudy was an Australian crocodile skin trader of German descent. He owned a chain of trade stores on the river. Twelve years before he had come to New Guinea as a patrol officer; for ten of those years he tracked the area. Eventually disgusted with administration red tape and uncertain future prospects of the service, he retired to Angoram. With his wife, he started a series of small businesses.

We asked him for suggestions of how we could see a bit of the Sepik River and its people before our plane was scheduled to depart for Wewak. Five days was a long time to fill and suggestions were slim. There really was not any place to go, except up or down the river by boat. He was planning to take his motorized canoe up the river that Monday in search of more crocodile skins. For the fee he requested, we jumped at the chance to go along. The trip would end at Pagwi, another trading post about two hundred miles up the Sepik. From there we could find land transport to Wewak. With Angoram as the alternative, we felt we had nothing to lose. We agreed to meet early Monday morning.

TAA
QANTAS

2-3. *Jackson's Airport*, Port Moresby, New Guinea's international airport (*left*) is jammed with travelers during the short midday period when all flights arrive and depart. The steeple of the city's St. Mary's Catholic Cathedral (*above*) is painted in the style typical of Maprik area spirit houses.

4. *A Bible class* early one ▶ Sunday morning in Port Moresby.

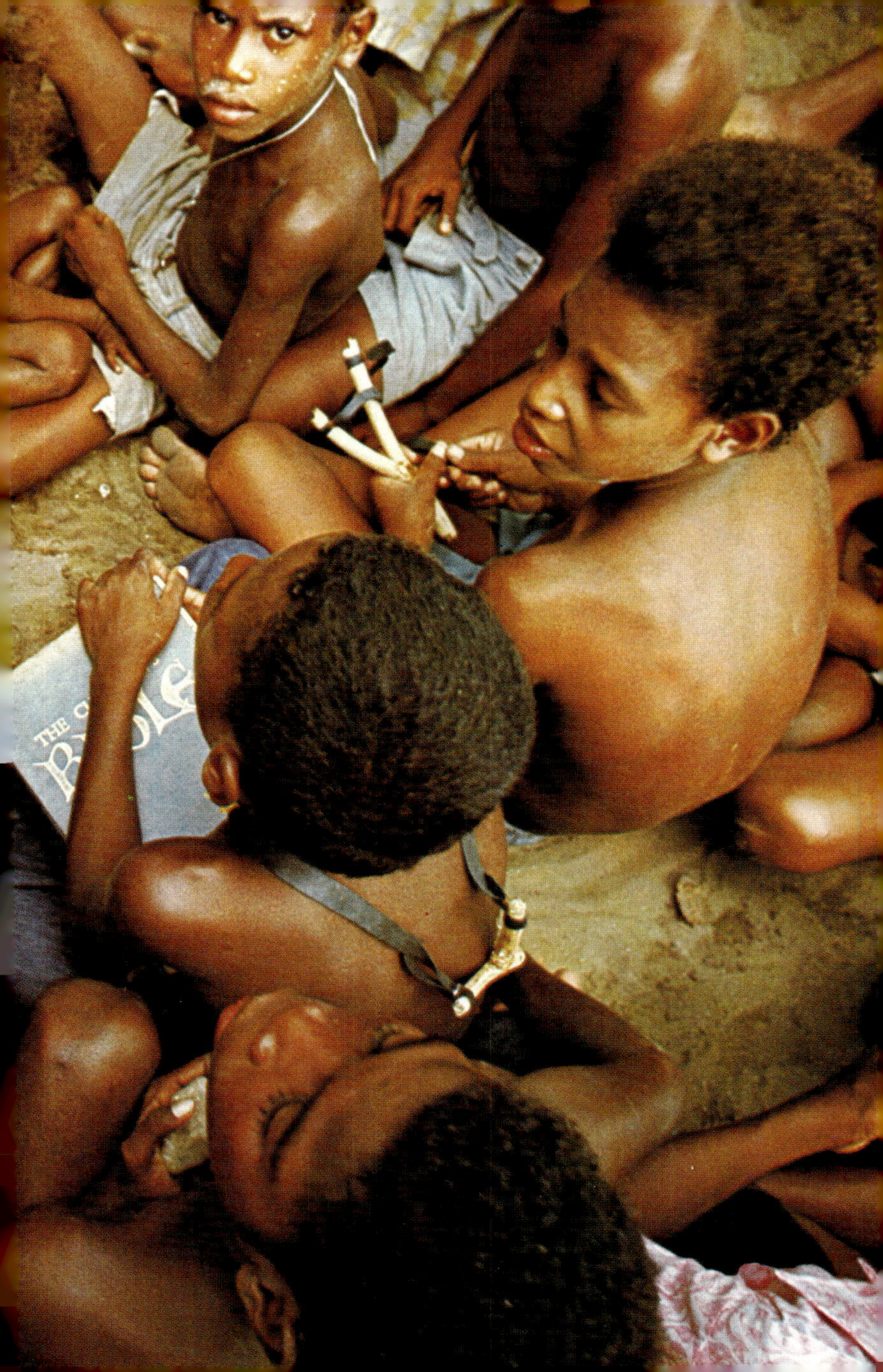
THE

5. *The ANG Building* in downtown Port Moresby is the tallest building in the Territory.

6. *Houses on stilts* built over the harbor are an answer to land shortage in the Port Moresby suburb of Hanuabada.

7. *The Salvation Army* holds a Sunday evening service in Koki Market in Port Moresby.

8. *Government nurseries* in Morobe District experiment with new varieties of trees in their search for suitable economic crops.

9. *Stately coconut palms* in orderly rows around St. Fidelis College in Alexishafen, Madang District, are typical of those on many plantations in the area.

10. *A round-house village* near Goroka is typical of the Eastern Highlands, built on a ridge as protection against animals and other tribes.

NEW GUINEA

11. *Bena Bena tribe girls* are noted for their bead handicrafts. The "New Guinea" belt worn by this girl, however, was bought from a trade store.

12. *Facial tattooing* is extremely ▶ popular among the women.

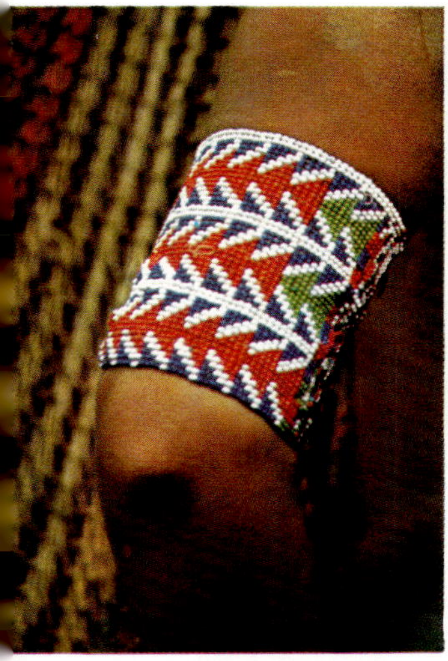

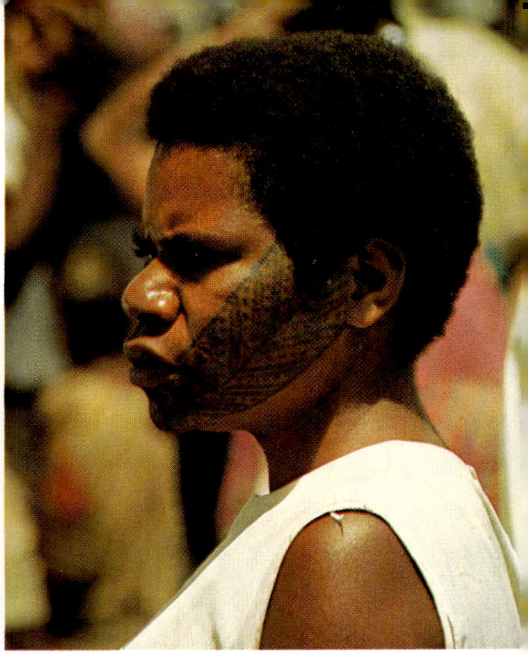

13-14. *A beaded band* worn at the public market in Goroka (*left*). Below, men take part in an economic development program that is teaching the technique of producing woolen products.

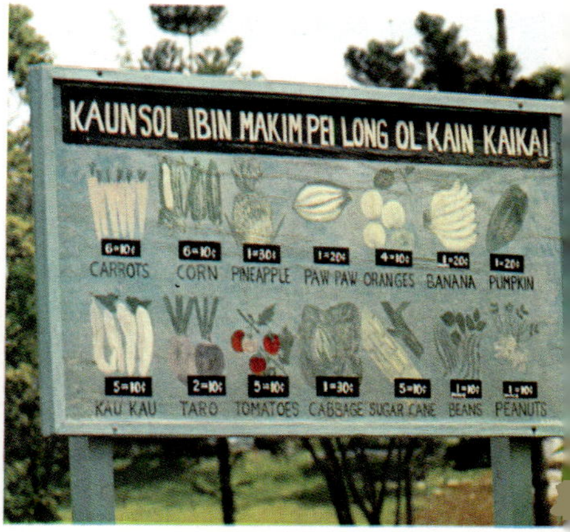

16. *Prices* at the markets are fixed by each local council, eliminating the necessity of bargaining.

15. *Market days* in Goroka are held on Wednesdays and Saturdays.

17. *The prized possessions* of this Daulo Pass woman are worn around her neck. They include beads, a rosary, a pocket knife, and a key. The latter is a great status symbol.

18. *Curious highlanders* from Daulo Pass pose willingly for a family portrait.

19. *A Bena Bena girl* sells pumpkins, pineapples, and corn in the Goroka market.

20. *Coffee*, grown on native-owned plantations, is weighed by the roadside near Goroka before delivery to the processing plant (*above right*).

21. *A village boy* from Wandi Village in Chimbu District on his way to a singsing.

22. *Pigs* are a New Guinean's most prized possession, and husbands and wives often stroll along the roads with their animals.

23. *The Highlands Highway* in Kundiawa, Chimbu District, probably offers the most beautiful scenery accessible by car.

24-25. *Spears* are not only ceremonial, they are routinely carried and used in the Highlands (*left*). Below, an eleven-year-old girl is dressed for her first singsing in an outfit of bird of paradise feathers, possum skins, and strung beads.

26-27. *Singsing preparations* in Wandi, Chimbu District. Decorative paints (*right*) are usually made from vegetable or other natural pigments. The young high school student above, however, preferred to use commercial paint from the local trade store.

28. *Ridge villages*, deep gorges, waterfalls, and endless mountains are seen on the ten minute flight from Goroka to Omkalai.

29. *Long houses* are built to house the many relatives who will arrive for the ceremony of pig killing.

30. *Kundu drums* are still hollowed out by burning out the center with hot rocks, even though the outsides are now shaped with modern steel tools.

31. *Husband and wife* attending a pig kill. The man is wearing a gold lip pearl oyster shell—a favorite bride price.

32-33. *Mother and child (left)* from the Western Highlands. A Meldpa man (*below*) sports a cuscus and cockatoo headdress.

34-36. *A local politician (left).* Leaves replace feathers when times are bad (*below*). Bamboo-stick necklaces (*opposite*) indicate wealth out on loan.

37. *Most natives* in the Territory still hunt their food with bow and arrow.

38-40. *The headdress* of the Asaro River Vally man (*below*) is adorned with cowrie shells. The mudmen (*right*) come from the same valley and perform an eerie, silent dance to commemorate a great victory over a neighboring clan.

42. *A pig kill* is one of the most festive occasions in any village. Villagers may spend a year in preparation.

41. *Tribesmen* near Kunduga learn how to use a radio. Administration radio stations provide news in tribal languages, cultural programs taped in nearby villages, and musical request shows.

43. *Most Highland markets*, like ▶ this one in Mount Hagen, serve as gathering places to meet friends in addition to selling large quantities of produce.

Sepik River Voyage

A multitude of rivers dissects New Guinea's terrain into islands of isolation—muddy rivers that hang from the mountains like greasy tresses of long hair begging for washing. Enormous rivers boil with turbulence during the rainy season and are hardly much tamer in the dry interval. If measured by volume of water, the Fly and Sepik Rivers are the largest. Born and fed in the Victor Emanuel Range, they meander in opposite directions like wriggling snakes through mountains and flat swamps. The Sepik flows north to the South Pacific Ocean, while the Fly heads south into the Gulf of Papua. Both are navigable for five hundred miles yet wander two hundred further.

Captain F.P. Blackwood, Royal Navy, discovered the Fly in 1845 while surveying the area on his flagship, the HMS *Fly*. Exploration was carried to its navigable limits by the Italian botanist D'Albertis in 1873. The Sepik was probably first ascended by Germans in 1880. Called the Kaiserin Augusta, it was well documented by various Germans who explored and traded along its banks. In 1920 an expedition headed by Charles Karius, explorer, and Ivan F. Champion, patrol officer, tracked the regions of both rivers. Their thrilling story of frustration and triumph is told in the understated book later written by Champion, *Across New Guinea from the Fly to the Sepik*. Champion was the first government representative to establish contact with the headhunting tribes inhabiting the area.

Missionaries have since tried to bring the river people into the twentieth century. The work on the Fly is especially difficult. One bush pilot who transports missionaries and their supplies into the area by seaplane described the place as "Unforgettable! The climate is miserable and the people disease ridden. It's a place only a missionary would venture." The Sepik, on the other hand, is well penetrated. Converts along the river and its channels have given up their tribal warfare and become slightly Westernized. People are slowly becoming interested in medical aid, new schools, and economic stability.

The latter is not easy. Crocodile skins used to be the main source of income, but overkilling has drastically reduced the reptile's once numerous population. New ecology laws prohibit importation of the skins into the United States, previously the largest buyer. With poor quality supply and a disappearing market, prices are rapidly dropping and the people are worried.

Few crops grow in the area: there are too many swamps and not enough solid ground. Starchy sago palm remains the basic staple in the diet. There are fish. This availability of protein probably contributed to the reason why the river people were basically headhunters and not cannibals. They never had an overpowering desire for meat.

As we left Angoram I dipped my hand into the Sepik's brown waters. It came out covered with fine grit. Bathing would be useless. Drinking was possible, but it would take a long time for all the mud to settle to the bottom of a cup. Fortunately, Rudy had packed ample rain water to satisfy our cooking requirements and lolly water to quench our thirst.

During the next six days we would be grateful for Rudy's skill. Confidently he avoided swirling eddies and floating debris. The river was no place for a novice. His knowledge was probably the reason his houseboat remained the only tourist hotel afloat. All the competition had inconveniently sunk at one time or another, usually loaded with guests.

Milton had brought a map from the government's Department of Land and Survey. It was not of much use. Continual shifting of the river caused old channels to close and new ones to open. Rudy had to rely on the current to tell whether or not each passage would go through. Banks were overgrown with *pitpit*, a form of wild sugar cane, which averaged about eighteen feet high. Like grass, the *pitpit* grew in dense profusion, making it impossible to see through or over it. We cut across the river continually. It was safer and faster to skirt the shore. This technique meant less chance of overturning and kept us out of the swift current. We wondered how we would hold up for the next few days in the open forty-foot motorized canoe. Already it looked like rain.

Kambaramba

We did not travel far, for darkness came early. It was necessary to make camp as soon as possible. When daylight ceased, all light ended. Electricity was nonexistent along the Sepik. Rudy pulled into a *barad*, or waterway, through a strip of land that connected one channel with the main stream. Kambaramba Village lay buried in the *pitpit*.

Kambaramba, we discovered, had a notoriously shady reputation. The people did not own land and had no other visible means of support. When they looked around for something to sell, women appeared to be the best solution. Kambaramba became a floating brothel. However, this village's major industry is unique in New Guinea. Prostitution is rare, and, unlike some cultures, a wife is never offered for liaison on a friendly basis with relative or stranger. New Guinea, therefore, was one of the few countries to escape World War II without producing a multitude of half-caste kids. As one American GI put it, "If you wanted to get out of the place alive, you never messed around with the women." Nevertheless, products of Kambaramba's labors of love hovered around our canoe in their pint-sized craft. They followed us to a rather shaky looking structure Rudy called the Haus Kiap. Every village has one. It provides housing for visiting government officials. Next door was a similar building that sheltered the accompanying policemen. We had obtained authorization from the administration to use these houses when available.

Lack of land forced the Kambarambans to build their homes over the channel instead of ground. Houses stand on posts about five feet above water. Sago palm trees provide much of the raw materials. Homes take three years to construct, for no usable timber grows nearby. Logs can only be floated downstream during flood season. Piles are laid the first year, floor and walls built the second, and roof and finishing touches applied the third. No one is inconvenienced by the lasped time. Homes are shared with neighbors and relatives until new buildings are completed. Split bark of the sago palm forms the floor. Pieces are laid crosswise on support beams beneath. We had to tread carefully. Centers were amply supported but ends often hung free. A careless step would flip the board up and deposit us directly into the channel below.

Eyes watched as we set up mosquito nets and laid out bed rolls. Gazes transferred to Rudy as he prepared dinner. "Never throw away empty bottles or cans," Rudy said. "The people always have uses for them." He stacked them neatly in a corner of the house and returned to his chores. Silently the refuse disappeared into the crowd.

It was still light when we finished dinner so we decided to canoe around the village. The older men had long since tired of looking at the strangers and had returned to their homes. Only *mankis* (pronounced monkeys), or young boys, formed our surrounding flotilla. It was amazing to watch how skillfully they handled their canoes. Games were formulated around our craft; who could outrace us, get the closest, or have their picture taken?

Their canoes sat about one inch above the waterline, and were hewn from a single piece of wood. Bows were tapered to a point and carved with a figure, generally a crocodile. The sides of the sterns were slightly curved but were left open at the rear, where they set almost flat on the water. The design allowed for cooking fires to be built there when canoes were taken on long journeys. People did not stop on shore to prepare food during a trip for fear they would be in enemy territory. Two types of paddles were favored. One shaped like a palm leaf was sufficient to maneuver in open channels and on the river. But a two-prong fork variety was necessary to push one's way through the overgrown *pitpit* frequently found blocking channels.

As landless people, Kambarambans not only have to live over no-man's-land but also farm floating gardens. Hunks of *pitpit* often break away from the mainland and float freely downstream. The Sepik is filled with such islands. Some attain an area of one-half acre. Often they move into channels, where, unless broken up and moved away, their climbing roots again knit them to the mainland. People scrutinize passing islands carefully. Occasionally a hapless wild pig happens to become its prisoner and their next meal. Some attach their canoes to substantial islands and float downstream without work. Others use them as fishing piers, since fish find the roots good cover. When enough soil is present to make the land farmable, the mass is tethered to a house and cultivated. Such free land becomes the property of the farmer. Instances have been reported, however, of farms mysteriously floating away in the night. Police investigations usually prove that a neighboring village has pulled off a land speculation deal.

A steady pounding noise led us to a group of women making sago. It appeared hard work for the small quantity gained. Considering the low food value, it is probably not worth the effort. After the bark of the sago palm was stripped away for building material, the center wood was handed over to the women. One sat pounding the wood into small pieces with a pickax. Another beat the pieces into a pulp with a long, thin stick. Water was run through the coarse pulp, which was then wrung out by hand. A trough system with a loose filter of woven reeds kept back any loose particles of pulp and passed the starch laden water through to a container below. Later the water would be drained off, leaving a mass of white gooey substance called sago in the bottom of the container. The sago was then rolled into balls and dried for storage.

Women prepare sago for eating by moistening the dried flour with a little water. Patted into flat tortilla shapes, sago is then fried over an open fire in a slightly curved clay pan. Pieces are eaten hot from the pan or carried rolled up in sacks until the hungry bush or river traveler might desire a bite. The only problem with sago is that it quickly becomes rancid, but because of the work involved in preparing it, sago is never destroyed, but eaten anyway.

We returned to the Haus Kiap and prepared for bed. The group of *mankis* that had trailed us around the village followed along to view the proceedings. Without the presence of elders they were quite bold. Every word we spoke came back in a mocking echo. Soon the repetitions resembled a chanting chorus. They giggled in delight at harassing us.

Tambunum

Daybreak was welcome. It was understandable why tuberculosis is so prevalent in New Guinea. We had spent a miserable night. Covers were tossed back and forth in an effort to escape the heat and chilly damp air that seeped in through the open floors. We spent little time preparing for our departure. Rudy knew Tambunum Village was a fair distance away and would require a full day's journey to reach. He was anxious to have us see what he called the "Ford assembly line of Sepik carvers."

We reached Tambunum's Haus Kiap as the sun was setting. It was a charming building constructed on the solid ground of the riverbank. Like the houses of Kambaramba, it was built on posts providing protection against sudden floods or roaming crocodiles. All the houses of Tambunum had curious faces thatched above their entrances. Eyes and noses were set over the openings while the doors sufficed for mouths to guard against evil spirits.

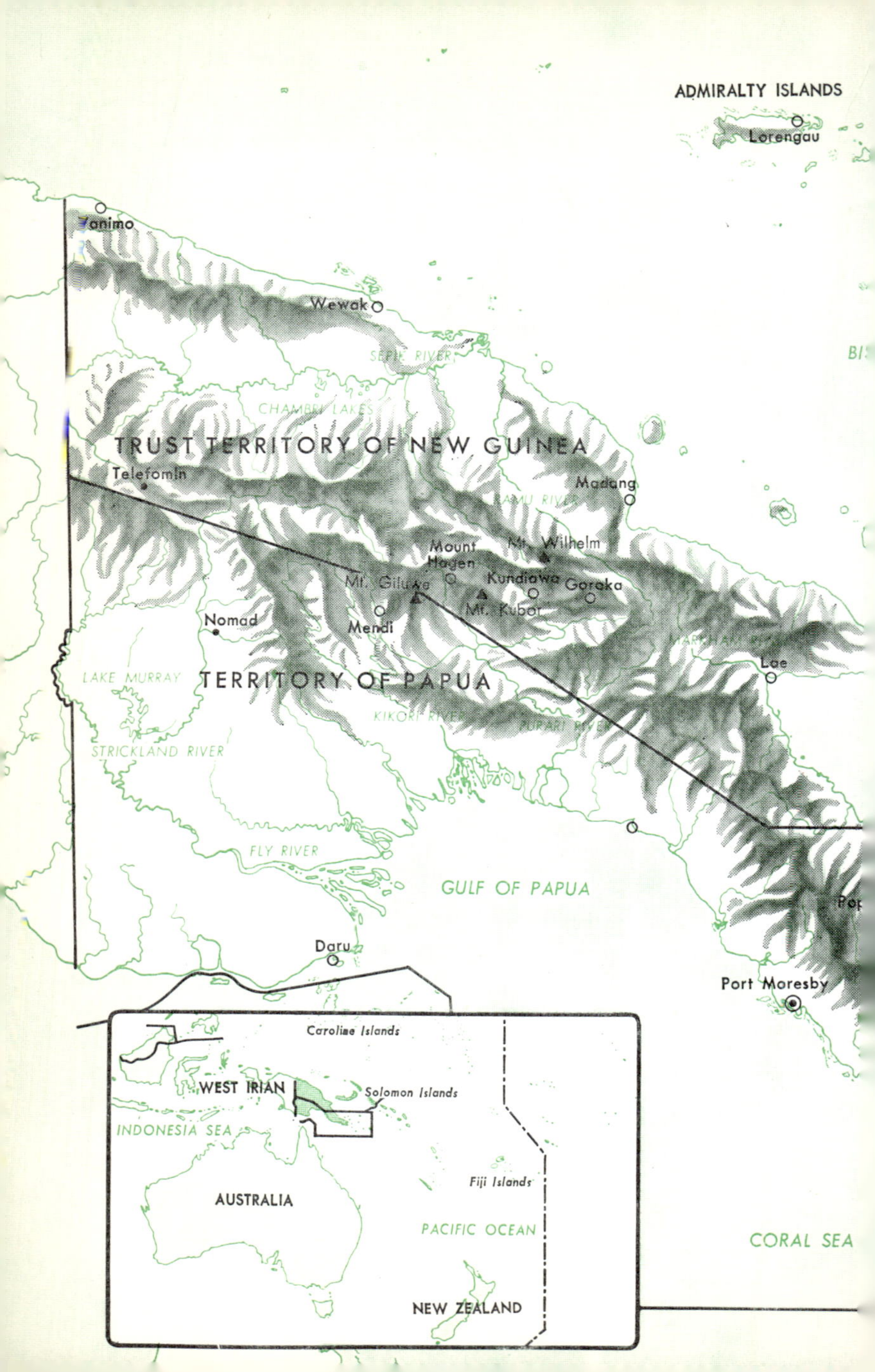

ADMIRALTY ISLANDS
Lorengau
Vanimo
Wewak
SEPIK RIVER
CHAMBRI LAKES
TRUST TERRITORY OF NEW GUINEA
Telefomin
Madang
RAMU RIVER
Mt. Wilhelm
Mount Hagen
Mt. Giluwe
Kundiawa
Goroka
Mt. Kubor
Mendi
Nomad
LAKE MURRAY
TERRITORY OF PAPUA
Lae
KIKORI RIVER
PURARI RIVER
STRICKLAND RIVER
FLY RIVER
GULF OF PAPUA
Daru
Port Moresby
CORAL SEA
Caroline Islands
WEST IRIAN
Solomon Islands
INDONESIA SEA
AUSTRALIA
Fiji Islands
PACIFIC OCEAN
NEW ZEALAND

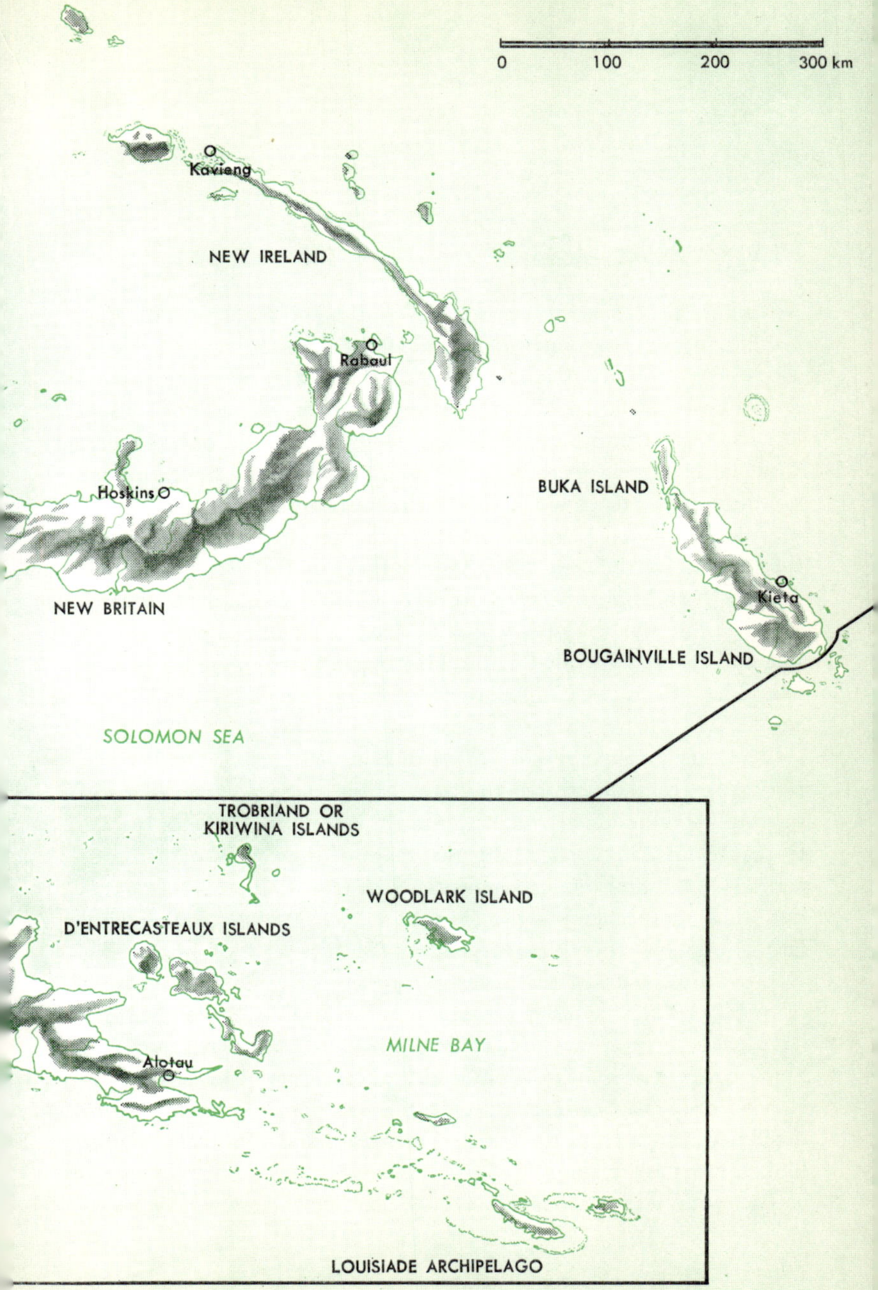
0
100
200
300 km
Kavieng
NEW IRELAND
Rabaul
Hoskins
NEW BRITAIN
BUKA ISLAND
Kieta
BOUGAINVILLE ISLAND
SOLOMON SEA
TROBRIAND OR
KIRIWINA ISLANDS
WOODLARK ISLAND
D'ENTRECASTEAUX ISLANDS
MILNE BAY
Alotau
LOUISIADE ARCHIPELAGO

NEW GUINEA

At one time Sepik carvers were considered the artists of New Guinea. Experts say most of the quality craftsmen have vanished. Artists of Tambunum were making a valiant effort to regain stature at the cost of the less discriminating tourists. Tambunum was a large village strung out for about three-quarters of a mile. Houses were fairly close together and two or three deep. Beneath each building sat a carver working industriously over a mask, figurine, or stool. Finished products hung from the rafters drying. There they waited for the next trader to pick them up for city curio shops. All masks and figurines were painted with vegetable dyes or earth colors. Lime was used for white, ground ocher mixed with sap for red, and charcoal blended with oil for black. Stools were for private use. They alone were aged over cooking fires until black from smoke.

The carvers appeared to be in a transitional period. Quality was not up to the standards of the past. Purists would argue that too many outside influences were ruining the designs. Yet if artists are to mature in competence and imagination, they need other influences. We did find one excellent craftsman, although his work was not truly middle Sepik style. He favored the Madang design with large birds or crocodiles carved on the forehead of his masks.

Government programs have been instituted to bring a measure of quality to New Guinea art. Missionaries and the United Nations have tried to promote interest in the pride of fine workmanship. Some curio dealers have supported their efforts and insist on purchasing only the best available. Of the few places concerned with quality, carvings from the Siassi, Trobriand, and Woodlark islands looked most promising.

Everyone was anxious to have us examine their work. We suspected it was more because we were prospective customers than guests. Truth became openly evident every time we turned over a work and found, in bold numbers, the asking price.

To our relief the peddlers disappeared silently when one man invited us into his home. The ladder did not look reliable, but we climbed up anyway. Once inside, the steps were pulled into the house. It was their way of keeping intruders out. True to New Guinea building style, the house lacked windows. It did have another door at the opposite end. When it was opened we had enough light to see the interior.

There was only one room. It was fairly large and cool. A cooking fire was in the center surrounded by a variety of kitchen utensils. Stone and metal adzes and hatchets appeared to be the basic work tools. Carved foot stools served as chairs, while wooden crates and metal biscuit tins provided tables. Two kerosene lamps furnished night light. We gingerly stepped on the rotting split-sago bark floor while gazing into the rafters. The family's collection of singsing and ceremonial gear hung from the beams.

Commercially made mosquito nets lay in various positions on the floor. They were suspended in space by strings tied to nearby posts and rafters. Our host pointed out one of traditional design. It was woven of grass reeds. The materials was similar to coarse burlap but about twice the thickness. We estimated its length to be about fifteen feet. Loops of cane held the baglike structure up inside to prevent the sides from touching the contents. At night the entire family and its pets retreated inside. Father came in last and closed the opening with rope. The closeness of unwashed bodies and the sweltering heat must have been unbearable. Yet it was better than facing hordes of bloodthirsty mosquitoes.

The *meri* of the house stood back looking wild eyed with a mixture of fear and curiosity. She never said a word, but only did what her husband directed. Signs of relief crossed her face as we prepared to leave. Scarcely were we down the ladder when we heard her chatting excitedly with an inquiring group standing below the back door.

Timbunke

Our first view of Timbunke rose out of the *pitpit* like a vision, which was quite appropriate considering it was the mission station. "French Catholic fathers," yelled Rudy as we passed the knot of whitewashed buildings. About a quarter mile later we turned into a half-hidden channel. The tall *pitpit* diminished rapidly to short-bladed grass. The channel continued wandering, slicing the village in half. Only a couple of precarious looking bridges connected the two portions. Their tied logs groaned under the weight of figures scurrying across to meet us at the landing.

Everyone eagerly welcomed Rudy. Before he even asked, many crocodile skins were produced. As he became engrossed in trading, we decided to stroll around the village. Several self-appointed guides left no blade of grass unturned in their effort to acquaint us with Timbunke's charms. It was a neat, picturesque little village. No matter which way we pointed the camera we found a photograph. Wood carvings and singsing paraphernalia were brought for our appreciation. Although the carvings were few, they did possess excellent workmanship. Timbunke's carvers seemed to emphasize quality instead of quantity.

Rudy was still trading when we returned to the boat landing.

We watched him measuring the skins with a ruler and figuring out payments. Handfuls of coins and salt were exchanged for the hides. Salt is a commodity as valuable as gold. Everyone kept his stock in tightly covered jars to prevent moisture from attacking it. Although some was used for seasoning, most was needed to cure fresh skins until the next passing trader could pick them up. As for money, Australian currency was used all over the Territory.

There used to be a silver coin minted strictly for New Guinea. Valued at one shilling (today, ten cents), the unique piece was pierced through its center. The hole made it convenient to string or store the cash on a stick. Whenever the administration purchased something, it paid for the goods with these coins either by the stick or pound: one stick equalled five dollars; one pound equalled twenty-five dollars. Not quite sure what money was all about in those days, the people either wore them for decoration or buried the cache. Eventually a coin shortage occurred. Today the New Guinea coin is no longer in circulation but a collector's prize.

Although they have learned its value, money is still somewhat strange to an indigenous's mind. Trade stores sell items for ten, twenty and thirty cents. We asked one manager why prices were not marked seven, twelve, or twenty-five cents. "I'd like to," he replied. "But they don't understand the value of pennies. Five cents is just beginning to be accepted." It was further reported that such change was tossed away.

It was late by the time Rudy salted the last of his purchases and buried them in the bow of the canoe. Too late to continue onward, he inquired the location of Timbunke's Haus Kiap. Pidgin directions informed us that accommodations were half a mile away. Our lodgings were located in the rear of the mission station. Our first foot on shore at the mission told us we should not have landed. It was immediately covered by mosquitoes. No amount of swatting deterred their effort to drain us dry. Flicking them off was useless. Desperately we applied more insect repellent. It helped, but some still bit through it. Neither Australia's nor the United States' finest insect repellents were effective for more than ninety minutes on the Sepik. We were continually reapplying the stuff. Efforts to rid ourselves of the pests were redoubled as dusk approached. Most mosquitoes were simply irritating, but after 5:00 P.M. the malarial variety started dining and we did not care to be their main course.

We found relief at the Haus Kiap. The malaria spray team had recently been through the area and coated the walls adequately with DDT. It was the six-month health insurance policy that drastically reduced cases of the disease. Some of the villages protested that the spraying increased the number of bedbugs. Spraying was stopped whenever the people dissented. Unfortunately bedbugs were the lesser of two evils. Usually within a month after the last remnants of DDT disappeared, cerebral malaria would again take the lives of village children. Of the three types of malaria in New Guinea, cerebral is the worst, an instant killer. The second variety has an incubation period of several months while the third takes almost a year to show up. We would be taking our antimalaria pills for a long time after departing New Guinea.

Chambri Lakes

We arose to bright sun. For the first time the threatening skies had disappeared, but we did not know if it was a blessing or not. While we kept moving in the canoe the wind provided a natural fan, but once on shore the humid heat enveloped us in a suffocating blanket of perspiration. We were promptly sunburned. Our route that morning left the river and struck out across swampland. The channels were alive with people canoeing. *Pitpit* resumed its normal stature and all traces of trees disappeared. Only flat green monotony remained as far as the eye could see. Occasionally a snowy white egret took our fancy, but it was always too distant to allow the pleasure of a thorough scrutiny. After a while, even the cooking fires on the sterns of passing canoes ceased to hold fascination. Finally the black channel waters began to turn dark blue and *pitpit* changed to water lilies. We had arrived at the marshes of Chambri Lakes. This area is covered with a chain of lakes connected to each other by swampy channels. Lake size increases or diminishes depending on the amount of rain. Fish, especially catfish, abound in the waters. Women in small canoes silently set out traps to capture them.

Aibon was our first stop. The village is famous for its pottery. Coarse-looking ware, it is traded up and down the river. Principal products included the flat sago frying pans and bowl-shaped open ovens used to hold fires. On the lighter side were water jugs, storage pots and flower vases, newly introduced by missionaries. All were covered with whimsical whitewashed faces, the trademark of Aibon.

The extremely coarse clay was shaped by the coil method. A sea shell with a large hole in its center was used to trim rough edges. This action often pulled up large stones from the surface of a pan. Picked out and tossed aside, the holes were filled with more clay. United Nations experts had taught the Chambri Lakes people better firing techniques. However, now that the teachers had left, the pupils resumed their old favorite of open flame firing. Consquently, the pottery was so brittle that only fifteen percent left the area without breaking.

The Haus Kiap at Lukluk was our hotel that night. It was probably the best built of any we stayed in. That meant the floor was in good condition. Lukluk did not appear a friendly place. The people were rather distant and kept to themselves, but Rudy liked them. He felt they were among the few river people who were not looking for something for nothing.

We watched the men in their meeting house across from the Haus Kiap. Curious welts circled their chests and backs. They were carved during a secret ceremony initiating them into manhood when they were young. The patterns were supposed to represent teeth marks of a crocodile. The men sat around the fire and played with a pet cassowary bird. The funny-looking creature could best be described as a brown-striped furry egg running around on two sticks.

Sunrise over the Chambri Lakes next morning was nothing short of spectacular. But we spent little time studying the changing colorwheel as our final destination was Pagwi, and it was still some distance away. Gusty winds whipped up the lake water to good sized swells. We never realized how turbulent things were until we left the shelter of Lukluk's last lily patch and tried to cross open water. Rudy quickly steered back into the nearest lily pads. The desired channel lay directly across the lake, but all of us vetoed the risk of trying to cross.

For two hours we amused ourselves by watching insects feed on the lily pads. We stopped dipping our hands overboard when Rudy announced it would be wiser if we did not. Crocodiles adored relaxing beneath the cooling lily leaves. Finally our patience gave out. Milton and Rudy decided to skirt the shore trying to stay in the sheltered waters of the lilies and floating grasslands. All went well until we entered the first grass field. Tightly knit roots soon tangled around the motor's propeller blades and halted the engine. Milton crawled onto the metal covered bow and began hacking away at the grass with a paddle. Unfortunately, Rudy had forgotten to bring his pronged fork version, which is considerably more suitable for the job. When Milton tore apart enough grass, Rudy revved the engine and plowed through the grass until the roots again halted the motor. Advancement was slow. It was over an hour before we reached open water, only to be tossed around by the still violent waves. A shaken Rudy swung the boat into the shelter of the nearest channel. We sat there until the wind died.

People in passing canoes were questioned as to whether or not the channel we wanted was still open. Each occupant nodded "yes" in agreement, so we headed across the lake to our destination. The deeper we penetrated the channel the narrower it became. Several times Rudy lost trace of a current. Then the channel ended. We backtracked a bit, found a new opening and continued, but this time it was blocked by a large island of *pitpit*. Rudy again backed out, found a new waterway and continued. Again and again the same thing happened. Rudy cursed his informants. Reaching another dead end, Milton attempted to stand up in the canoe. He hoped to see over the *pitpit*, which at this point was about six feet high.

When he stated that he saw another channel about twenty-five feet away beyond the strip of *pitpit*, Rudy decided to try and crash through the mess rather than skirting it. As soon as Milton resituated himself on the bottom of the canoe, Rudy ran up the engines to full power and jammed the boat into what looked like a slim opening in the roots. We managed to move about three feet, collect a boat load of red ants, receive several cuts from the razor-sharp grass, and disturb a swarm of hungry mosquitoes.

In between swatting, Milton and Rudy decided they could make it. Rudy manned the rear engine, and Milton went to the bow again with the paddle to repeat the grassland routine. For over an hour they hacked and rammed while I eliminated the mosquitoes, ants, spiders, and one lone centipede. One last concerted effort and we were haggard, cut, and exhausted but free. Ripples of current told us we had finally found the main channel. We would have little more trouble, but the dock at Pagwi was now another day away.

As the sun began to lower, birds gathered in large flocks. Ducks, egrets, herons, and others appeared more tame in this channel and allowed us to approach as close as twenty feet before taking flight. Once one started they all rose in a thunder that drowned out the noise of our engine. Thousands circled overhead until fear subsided, then they fluttered to the earth.

Black channel water gave the delicately bent *pitpit* a mirror image in which to study its reflection. Excitingly graceful geometric patterns passed in exhibition. It was an exquisite finale to a difficult but worthwhile day.

Kanganaman

I took a while to recover from my triumphant entry into Kanganaman, when I slipped off the riverbank and ended up standing in Sepik mud up to my thighs, but eventually I was ready for a visit to the Haus Tambaran. The one at Kanganaman was considered so fine that the administration has declared it a national treasure. The village capitalized on the event and charges visitors fifty cents each to see it.

A *tambaran* is a spirit. It can be good or evil. Hopefully it is good, but if it is not properly cared for it could go the other way. A Haus Tambaran, then, is a place for the spirit to dwell. They are strictly for men. Women are never allowed to enter—unless they are white and possess fifty cents. Since white magic is considered different from black, all the rules of the game change accordingly. This is the reason why it is foolish to spend time trying to convince natives that their beliefs are superstitious. Our magic protects us from the things that could happen to them. During an initiation ceremony in the Haus Tambaran, all indigenous women are not even permitted close to the building. Some villages refuse permission even at other times for women to walk past the structure. They must crawl. Penalty for a violation is death.

Kanganaman's Haus Tambaran is about two hundred feet in length. Its center is about twenty feet in height, rising to sixty in the front and rear. The overall appearance was made to represent open crocodile jaws. Intricately carved posts attested to its old age. Each post was a different pattern, depicting men, gods, devils, birds, and crocodiles. The building was a museum not only in its construction but also because of the ceremonial artifacts it contained. Wooden drums, flutes, masks, weapons, and stools decorated the downstairs. Singsing equipment of woven grasses was stored on the second floor.

Everyone reminisced about the good old days; fighting days, when a man proved he was so by warring with his enemies. Rudy had witnessed a canoe battle once, and said they were excellent fighters. The weapon he most admired was the spear thrower. It

44. *Young boys*, known in pidgin as ▶ *mankis* (pronounced monkeys) become adept at handling canoes on the Sepik River at an early age.

was a piece of cutout bamboo in which the implement was lodged. With a flick of a wrist the spear was projected from its mount with fearsome speed.

"They used to fight in long canoes," he related. "Large shields in the front of the boat protected the crew from injury. Behind the shields on either side stood two men with spear throwers. They sent out a terrific barrage of missiles. If a man was hurt, he was knocked off and another quickly took his place. When they approached the enemy at closer range, middlemen took over and fired arrows. Finally as they drew broadside, the rear crew finished the job with clubs in hand-to-hand combat."

Headhunting was the object of their battles, for a Haus Tambaran could not be erected until each post was wet with the blood of an enemy. Heads taken were saved as trophies. Those of slain comrades were kept as sacred. Both were stored inside the Haus Tambaran. The skin was pulled off by the teeth of the victorious. Clay was then packed over the skull to replace the missing skin. Hair of the victim and shells filled in the features.

None of those relics could be seen in Kanganaman's Haus Kiap. Most had been sold to the curious or museums. In a move to abolish warfare, the administration had put a ban on their export. Yet there were rumbles that if we were interested one might be found. We ignored the opportunity. We held the feeling that the indigenous had learned the value of a dollar too well, and, with today's cost of living, it did not seem reasonable to have someone lose his head over a couple of dollars.

45. *The first step* in the preparation of a dugout canoe being made in Kambaramba Village on the Sepik River.

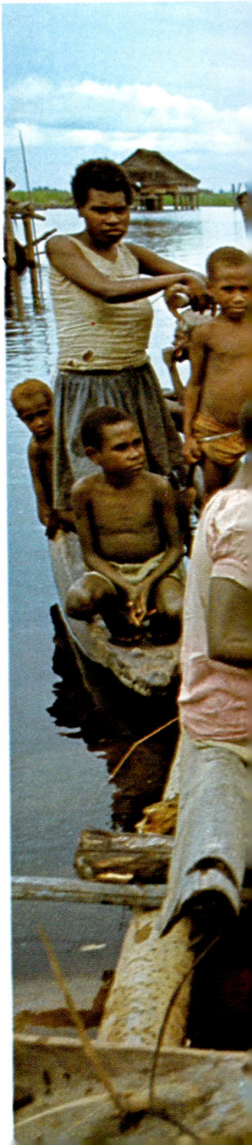

46. *Sago* is a principal food of the lowland people. The heart of the sago palm is chopped into fine pieces (woman on left), and then beaten into pulp (woman on right).

47. *Wood carvers* and other Sepik ▶ families live and work beneath their houses to avoid the heat of the tropical sun.

48. *A log bridge* spans the stream that divides Timbunke Village.

49. *A covered footbridge* of unusually good construction in Kanganaman Village on the Sepik River.

50. *Tambanum Village*, Sepik River. Homes in the Eastern Sepik District are large and, like most New Guinea houses, are without windows.

51. *Luluk Village* is located on ▶ a small, quiet island in the Chambri Lakes. This spot would be paradise, if it were not for the swarms of mosquitoes.

52. *Coconut milk* provides a refreshing drink in places where drinking the water can be a hazardous pleasure.

54. *Sepik River boys* are ▶ marked with crocodile patterns as they come of age.

53. *Mosquito netting* is a vital prerequisite to camping along the Sepik River.

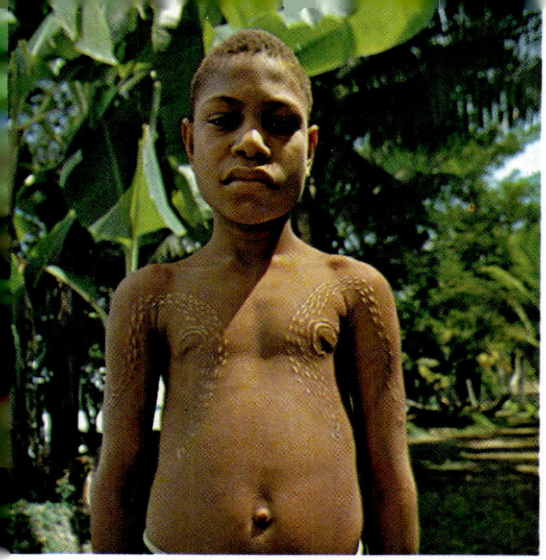

56. *A dance mask* suspended from the ceiling of a Haus Tambaran in Timbunke Village on the Sepik River. ▶

55. *A typical trade store* carries a variety of inexpensive goods, produced mostly in mainland China.

57. *Between singsings* the ceremonial masks usually hang on the upper level of Haus Tambarans.

58. *In the Chambri Lakes* region masks are often made from clay. This one also incorporates wrappers from cans of Japanese 777 brand mackerel.

59. *Intricately carved posts* support the most important Haus Tambarans in the Sepik River region.

60. *Most ceremonial masks* are either carved from wood or woven from reeds. Note the colorful tin plate incorporated into this mask.

63. *Fish traps* are the most popular method used for gathering daily protein along the Sepik River.

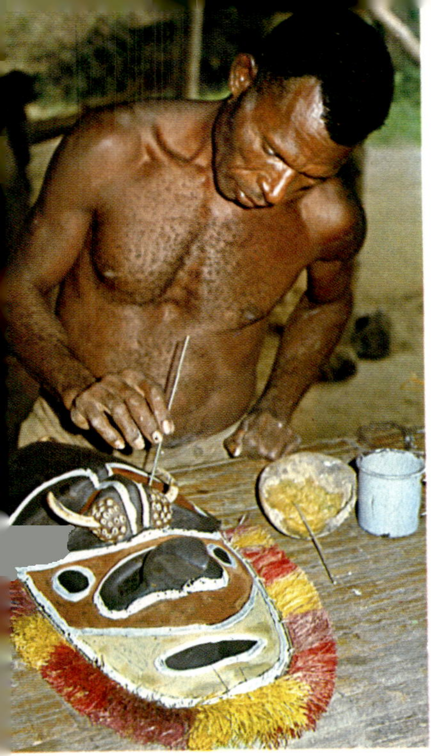

61. *Tourists* have created a demand for bright, simply made wooden masks, thereby providing an increasing income to villagers far from the souvenir shops.

62. *Increasing demand* by tourists for traditional Sepik River masks has reduced the art to a mass production process.

64. *Pottery cooking utensils* made in Aibon Village are smoothed with a seashell tool.

65. *A moist, coarse clay* is used by Aibon potters. Two weeks of drying are required before firing.

56. *Aibon pottery* is known for its multiple faces. However, because of poor firing techniques it is so fragile that it is rarely seen outside the Sepik River region.

57. *Sago* is almost totally starch and has little food value. A favorite method of preparation is to fry it in flat, moist cakes.

70. *Women* do most of the fishing in the Chambri Lakes region. Their catch is usually catfish. ▶

68. *Wild sugarcane,* called "pitpit," grows to great heights along the Sepik River. Lacking sweetness, it is of little use.

69. *Pitpit* in large masses often floats freely on the Sepik River. Canoeists sometimes must hack their way through blocked channels.

◀71. *Rudy Treutlein* runs his outboard powered dugout canoe up the Sepik River in search of crocodile skins. The forty-four-gallon drum contains his fuel supply.

Back to the Coast

WEWAK

After six threatening days, promises of rain were finally fulfilled just as the last of our equipment found its way onto the dock at Pagwi. We splashed our way through slowly rising puddles to the dry porch of a riverfront trade store. Supposedly there was a bus from Pagwi to Wewak. No one huddled on the porch was sure of its whereabouts. Milton and Rudy trotted off to make further inquiries but received only sketchy information. Everyone did agree that the road was in very bad condition since it had been raining for several days. The news was disappointing. After six days of roughing it, the prospect of a clean bed and bath was a fancy that my mind dwelled upon at length. Luckly two Catholic fathers were organizing plans for a truck to transport children to a mission school in Wewak. They offered to inform the truck driver to give us a lift but apologized for not knowing what time the vehicle would arrive.

With our onward arrangements settled, Rudy decided to depart. He bought a box of large-size disposable plastic garbage bags. Carefully tearing holes in the bottom and two sides of one of the bags, he turned it upside down and slipped it over his head. Then with the air of a man who just purchased a two-hundred-dollar raincoat, he waved and left. We finally lost sight of his canoe as it meandered downstream. Quite a man, Rudy. One who took intense pleasure in possessing the brains and imagination to survive the rigors of the area.

Now there was nothing left to do but wait. Puddles rose and fell with the intensity of the rain. Dinner consisted of two cans of cold spaghetti. It was the only item in the limited stock of the trade store that did not require cooking. We waited some more, until at last excited voices and the sound of a motor announced the arrival of our transport. It was nearly 6:00 P.M. Darkness was beginning to settle. Through the fine drizzle we saw our future chariot to civilization. We had ridden in many vehicles before but a dump truck was a novelty.

It was seven before the truck was ready. The driver had decided we should occupy the seat of honor. Our knapsack was tied securely in the rear while the rest of our gear was crammed into the small cab with us. We settled ourselves as comfortably as possible within the confines of the tiny space. Everyone assured us the trip was but a few hours. For such a short length of time, the crowding could be endured. The truck started with a jolt, drove a few yards and stopped. Petrol was the only object missing. It took the gas station attendent and driver another half hour to fill the tank. Fuel was siphoned from a forty-four-gallon drum to five-gallon pails, which were then poured into the fuel tank. Half an hour was not bad considering we were in a ten-ton truck.

Road conditions had been considerably understated. Mud the consistency of lard caused the truck to slide and slip continuously. Constant jogging lulled our senses into a semiconscious state. Cramps began setting in from tense muscles. Most of the difficulty of the bone-crushing ride came from the fact that the large vehicle was empty. Every bump thrust the truck up and down like a bouncing ball.

We stopped frequently, sometimes so the driver could chat with a *wantok*, sometimes to pick up students. The level of squeaky voices coming from the rear increased rapidly. We wondered what sort of fears were rifling through their minds: a cold wet ride; no chance of seeing friends and relatives for the next year; going into a strange world of unfamiliar spirits, devils, and tribes. Education must be very important to young people who braved so much to obtain it.

Around 1:00 A.M. our truck was flagged down in a small village. People talked excitedly with the driver. "Bris [bridge] he bagarap" was about the only phrase we could understand. After continuing on we tried to ask the driver if a washed-out bridge lay ahead, but our efforts were futile. He failed to understand our broken Pidgin questions. We rumbled on for a little while before stopping again. This time the driver was tired and wanted to rest in the bush. From the other passengers we continued to overhear rumors of an approaching problem.

The short term nap was followed by an even shorter drive into a large village. Cars were parked along the highway the entire length of the community. A figure running out to stop us confirmed the report that a washed-out bridge was indeed just ahead. The driver turned to us. "We wait. Half past two river okay." The bridge was actually a concrete ford. It was not washed out; simply under a deep torrent of rushing water. Though no one else had tried, our driver decided we could make it. Slowly we dipped into the rushing rapids. Water licked around the steps of the cab trying to sweep us into the fiercely bubbling foam below the concrete slab. But the driver pushed the vehicle steadily forward at a slight angle into the turbulence until the wheels gripped the mud of the opposite embankment.

It was 4:30 in the morning when we reached Wewak. On the outskirts of town was a hotel a friend had recommended as the best. We ignored its blackened interior and requested the driver to dump us on the doorstep. After the motor noise disappeared in the night, the sound of waves pounding on the beach took over. For half an hour Milton tried to raise the management to no avail. In his wanderings he did discover that the place had outdoor toilet and shower facilities complete with towels. So we moved our belongings to a sheltered area and partook in the luxury of hot baths and genuine Western-style toilets, minus mosquitoes, chickens, and the crowning touches of the Sepik.

Madang

Flying Ansett from Wewak to Madang was pleasant for two reasons: it gave our highway racked bodies time to relax and provided an aerial view of what everyone considered to be the loveliest town in the country. Channels separated the numerous specks of islands in Astrolabe Bay from the mainland. Slivers of water also sliced sections of the mainland, giving the town the overall appearance of Venice. But Madang's scenic value was not completely spent on the geometric patterns of aerial views. Coronation Drive along the coastline was dotted with attractive hotels and a beautiful nine-hole golf course whose water traps were covered with lilies.

Many of the town's residents had retired to the area. The atmosphere was slow and easy. Relationships between blacks and whites were unusually good. Economy may have had something to do with it. Cocoa plantations provided the principal income. They paid off quite well to indigenous owners, and not all of the profits were drunk up. Much of the cash supported expatriot owned shops in town.

Our home for the first few days was the Madang Christian Women's Association cottage. CWA cottages were located all over the country. Originally they were designed to provide low-cost housing for pregnant women to live in while waiting for delivery. It was a comfortable haven for us. However, two days after our arrival an expectant mother came. Since she had first choice on rooms, we had to leave. Although the costs were three times that of the CWA cottage, we had no complaint about the Hotel Madang. Rates included full board and a superb Chinese cook who even knew his pastries. The management ran a continental style establishment with not only excellent cuisine but outstanding service too, a rare find in New Guinea.

Once resettled, we continued sightseeing. Of all the outlying suburban villages, Yabob and Bilbil were the most interesting. Both are pottery centers. Like Aibon of Chambri Lakes, the main effort went into the manufacturing of pots and pans. Unlike Aibon, finished products were well made. Part of the reason for quality was a finer clay. Madang area potters also heeded the wisdom of kiln firing taught by their United Nations teachers. The work resembled terracotta in texture, with a slight natural glaze obtained from the type of clay used.

Although potter's wheels were available at both villages, they appeared unused. Artists preferred to take a ball of clay and repeatedly toss a smooth stone into its center until the traditional round shaped pot had been pounded inside out. Hands confidently formed the exterior and rim until a thrown look was achieved. Clay was packed tightly by beating a stick on the exterior every few days. This also drove out moisture so the pot could dry before firing. However, the clay of the area was so wet that it took two to four weeks for a piece to dry.

Designs were incised near the end of the drying time by means of a pointed *mamboo* (bamboo) stick. Yabob's top artist, Liton, made deep, sharp cuts. Ancient village marks were used as the basic patterns, which never varied in design. Bilbil people incised their pots with lighter, plainer marks. All were original designs and looked similar to tattoo patterns.

Women were the principal craftsmen, mainly widows or old *meris* with plenty of extra time. Business was good and was turning these women into wealthy people. The men were jealous, especially since the *meris* fought viciously to keep their new-found wealth to themselves. Taunted by the ladies into trying their hand at the craft, the men would occasionally work a pot. Instead of the fifty-cent price asked by the women, men tagged their item for five dollars. Anything made by a man was always considered more valuable regardless of quality.

Rabaul

Rabaul has a history that is as explosive as its surrounding volcanoes. It is situated on the Gazelle Peninsula on the northeast tip of New Guinea's second largest island, New Britain.

In the local Gunantuna language, Rabaul means "mangrove," a tree that grew profusely in the surrounding tidal swamps. Credit for draining the swamps and erecting a town of charming buildings and boulevards goes to the Germans. They needed a port close to their massive coconut plantations from which they could ship copra to the markets of the world. Until 1914 Rabaul was the German capital of the Territory. After World War I a League of Nations mandate gave Australia the right to administer former German New Guinea. Because of its central location, the Australians chose Lae for their future capital. However, before the final move could be made, World War II had begun. Hastily Port Moresby was given the honor, which it still retains.

World War II left more scars in Rabaul than any place else in the Territory. Once considered the loveliest town in New Guinea, it was totally destroyed. Many old-timers feel it is just beginning to regain its former charm. Boats are still found intact in the caves along Tavui Beach where the Japanese used to hide them to avoid Allied bombs. Japanese headquarters can be seen in a concrete cave beneath downtown. Military maps incised on the walls are clearly readable to any one who understands the language. Simpson Harbor and nearby plantations are dotted with rusting memorabilia; ships, heavy construction equipment, fighters, and bombers lie half covered in water or brush.

But not all destruction was wrought by war. Rabaul and volcanoes are synonymous. A semicircle of them hems Simpson Harbor. They loom ominously in the background from any vantage point in town. Matupit, sometimes called Tavurvur, is the most active. Recorded history shows it exploded in 1767, 1378, 1937, 1941, and 1942. It is still rumbling and spewing ashes. A volcanologic observatory on the rim of its crater keeps watch over the activity.

A favorite highlight of the area is the public market every Wednesday and Saturday. It is the largest in the Territory in regard to the quantity and variety of produce offered. Crowds and merchandise cover practically every available inch of space and make walking difficult. Yet for its immense size only about half the people interested in selling produce are visible. The other half sits a few blocks away. They are members of the Mataungan Association, who boycotted the public market and set up one of their own. Their crusade against white domination has earned them the title "Rabaul Rousers."

The Mataungan Association is a militant, fiercely antiwhite organization that controls much of the population of Gazelle Peninsula. Its members are the Tolai people. Most are independently wealthy from their own coconut and cocoa plantations. Profits are often enough to allow them the luxury of hiring laborers from other New Guinea tribes to work their fields. Some own trade stores and small industries and have learned the value of not giving away their stock.

Besides running the cooperative market, the association sets and collects its own taxes and makes laws in direct competition with the administation. It is a fairly young organization, which grew rapidly after World War II. Some Europeans are convinced that American GIs stationed in Rabaul started the entire movement. Flagrant American spending and equal rights ideals moved a few indigenous leaders into starting so-called cargo cults.

Americans, like other foreigners living in New Guinea, appeared to the local people to receive goods from incoming ships as if they were gifts. Soon the Tolai leaders began wondering why some of the arriving cargo did not come to them. One of the leaders formally announced that a shipment of free goods just for New Guineans would soon arrive. The people became excited, dropped their gardening tools, and haunted the harbor waiting for their ship to come in. Administration people became worried. Ignoring gardens meant the people would starve. Publicly they cornered the Tolai leader and demanded he name a specific date for the ship's arrival. When the date came and went and nothing happened, the cult was temporarily halted. Discredited, the leader dropped from view. A few years later cargo cults cropped up again. The cargo's failure to arrive this time was blamed on the Europeans. Their white magic erased Tolai names and replaced them with European ones on crates of goods shortly before they were unloaded.

Variations on the theme have popped up all over the country since then. In the interior, planes are worshiped as giant birds that bring cargo. Christianity is sometimes seen as a shortcut to cargo, since boxes are always coming to missions from outside sources. The idea of donations from people in other countries is not understood. Some missionaries suspect the willingness of natives to become nuns or priests is motivated by the expectation of a quick fortune.

But the Tolai are not the only people inhabiting the area. Another group that fits well into Rabaul's life-style are the Bainings. Among their accomplishments is firewalking in New Guinea style. We learned that a Baining village was planning an authentic singsing late Saturday night. Rabaul Excursions was going to take a small group of privileged tourists and offered us the opportunity to go along.

Mass confusion was in control when we reached the site. Off to one side sat a large group of guitar and ukelele strumming youths. New Guinea's answer to Woodstock was filled with writhing youngsters who loved dancing to modern country and western tunes of a string band. Opposite the string band sat older people beating out rhythms by pounding long shafts of bamboo on a piece of the same material lying on the ground. Chants accompanied the drone of drums.

An hour elapsed before the bonfire was built for the dance. We welcomed the fire not only as a signal for the performance to commence but because it provided warmth. Without sweaters, the night air proved chilling. Sparks exploded from the blaze whenever pieces of wet wood were licked with flames. Showers of fire glistened in the eyes of the children gathered around the blaze in agitated mirth. In a succession of leaping flames and smoldering ashes the fire increased and decreased in intensity, while we waited for the performers to arrive.

Dressing for the performance was a long and arduous task. Costumes were donned deep in the bush away from the eyes of women. Strange masks of pounded bark cloth worked into animal and bird shapes were the most popular. Other dancers wore creations of sewn leaves on giant frames resembling insects and butterflies. Bodies were covered with black grease, and clumps of grass were tied around arms and ankles. Only the soles of feet remained bare.

No one could explain the exact connotations of their fire dancing. All we could learn was that it represented a sexual rite. When all the performers were ready, they came prancing silently out of the bush. By the time they reached the glare of the bonfire, their tempo had quickened to a frenzy. The string band ceased, and everyone came running in our direction. More wood was added to the fire.

Performers began jumping into the air with excitement. Suddenly one man ran directly into the blaze. A rain of sparks descended on participants and audience as the flames burst like exploding fireworks. Another man danced through, kicking the glowing red wood high into the air. The crowd became ecstatic. Armfuls of sticks were continually fed to the blaze. Whenever it became intense enough, more men danced through it. Worked up by the excitement, members of the audience began joining the dancers. Even a small boy frolicked in the blaze until he clashed with a performer and was pulled back into the crowd by onlookers.

Unfortunately we only saw five short dances of the first part of the ritual before the tourists in our party became anxious to leave. Half said it was too late, while the others argued that the crowd was uncontrollable. We could not deny it was late, but the crowd was hardly unrestrainable since many younger people had already returned to dance with the string band. We were annoyed that the visitors in our group could not fully appreciate the opportunity.

Daru

Among the people we had met in Rabaul was Paul Cox. We enjoyed Paul because he enjoyed life. People of any color were a delight to him and he was filled with tales of his associations with everyone he had met in New Guinea. With only a few more days left in New Guinea, we asked Paul where he thought we could spend the remaining time wisely. "Daru" was his one-word reply. It took two long flights to reach the small island off the south coast of Papua near the mouth of the Fly River. Besides being the name of the tiny speck of land, Daru was also the name of its only town.

Daru serves as headquarters for the Western District. This area has the unique distinction of being the least explored and most primitive in the entire country. Stone axes are continually taken from cannibals still active in the Nomad area. Government attempts to stop the practice have met with little success. Those who are caught are sent by air to Port Moresby for trial.

Justice in New Guinea is strange. Few natives have an understanding of Western jurisprudence. They treat the most serious crime rather lightly, for to a New Guinean's way of thinking, no crime has been committed. A cannibal's defense attorney will plead that he was acting properly according to his traditional customs. Prosecution usually wins in the end, however, for Western law, the current law of the land, forbids the taking of human life, as a cultural trait or otherwise. Sentences are short and offenders are soon returned to their tribes. The administration hopes that they will learn by this lesson. In reality it appears that it simply gives them an experience that they can brag about for years to come.

Everything entering the district goes through Daru. That includes not only oil and copper explorers but supplies and food for those living in the area. Because the island is so remote from domestic transportation, goods are shipped directly from Australia as opposed to normal routes through Port Moresby.

Despite its inaccessibility, local people are used to contact with foreigners. Daru had been a stopping place for Malaysian and Portuguese trading vessels long before any other Europeans established colonies in the country. With such a historic record of tourists, one expects Daru to be much visited. Yet it remains relatively unknown. The only measureable fame occurred when the Indonesians were making war preparations on the West Irian border several years ago. Australia selected Daru as a supply base and built a military airstrip and a hospital capable of handling a large number of casualties. When nothing evolved, the airstrip was left to rapidly growing grass, while the hospital remained the best equipped but least inhabited in the Territory.

There was one hotel on the island. It had recently changed management and was undergoing renovations. Meal times more than made up for inconveniences incurred by the construction crews. Baramundi, a tasty saltwater fish caught in abundance in the surrounding waters, was the main course. When in season, baramundi provides the area with a new industry to replace the dwindling crocodile skin trade.

Paul Cox had arranged for his good friend John Smeeten to meet us at the airport. John was a large, gray-haired, jolly man, who immediately offered to be our personal guide. The first point of interest he showed us was Radio Daru, where he was Chief Administrator. He was preparing his indigenous staff to take over the operation in the near future.

Radio Daru, and all other radio stations in the Territory, except for scattered stations of the Australian Broadcasting Company, are operated by the administration. Programming is relatively simple. Musical request shows are the principal attraction. Listeners send in their proposals and selections are played on the air. The rest of the agenda consists of news broadcasts several times daily in a selection of different local languages, singsings tape recorded in villages of the district and played in an effort to bind the area together culturally, educationally oriented programs, and occasional music from other Pacific islands.

Radio stations provide the only true communication network throughout the inaccessible country. Police patrols distribute radios to villages that do not have one. Someone in each village is taught how to use the radio and replace the batteries. When disaster strikes or district headquarters wants to give instructions to some individual, the announcement is sent over the air. "It never fails to work," related John. "Even the most remote villager eventually gets the message and takes proper action." It is unlikely that many other radio services around the world have developed such confidence in their audiences.

"Speaking of people," continued John, "you must meet George Craig. He's a true Australian gentleman!" George was more than just a gentleman. He was a former crocodile hunter turned conservationist. After years of hunting he had grown to admire the beasts. Realizing that their population was dwindling, he decided to attempt to capture them alive. "I tied a beaut to the side of my boat," he related. "By the time I reached Daru the creature had drowned. To bring one back alive became a bigger challenge than I expected." Eventually he was successful, as we were to see.

We followed George to his backyard and into a large wooden structure. "Stand back," he commanded as he slowly drew open a wooden panel. We peeped through the opening, then rapidly retreated. We had not been prepared to see two beady eyes sitting on top of a long, half-opened snout full of sharp pointed teeth staring back at us. Our next look was more cautious. "Though they appear to be slow, they are extremely fast," explained George. To demonstrate, he produced a bucket of fish and tossed them one at a time to the prehistoric creature. Instantly the crocodile flipped his head completely on its side and snapped his jaws together. The fish disappeared in two gulps. Collecting food in this amusing way is a necessity, because crocodiles have rigid lower jaws. "He only has side vision," George further explained. A fish dropped directly in front of him went ignored while he eagerly snapped up others thrown to either side. Considering his eighteen-foot size we were amazed at the agility the reptile possessed.

While his wife, Shirley, served coffee, we sat and looked at George's photo album. It principally depicted his early crocodile hunting days. George expressed only admiration for the one-time foe he had avidly hunted. He spoke of them as a man would of a woman with whom he was enmeshed in a passionate love affair. Through George's eyes we learned to appreciate crocodiles not as ugly monsters but as beautiful wild beasts.

George's crocodiles had rounded out our educational film on New Guinea. We considered our work completed and prepared to leave. Before putting his camera away, Milton saw an opportunity to photograph a cute *pikinini*. With the mother's permission he pointed the camera in the direction of the happy child. Tears formed instantly and the child disappeared into the folds of his mother's dress. He refused to show his face. "Guess I should have warned you," said John. "Remember when you were a kid and your mother said if you weren't good the bogyman would get you? Here the indigenous say the same thing to their children. Only the bogy isn't some nondescript creature of undetermined origin. Here he's just white."

BIBLIOGRAPHY

A Traveler's Guide to Papua New Guinea. Ann Mallard. Jacaranda Press Pty., Ltd., Australia

Across New Guinea from the Fly to the Sepik. Ivan F. Champion. Landsdowne Press, Melbourne

Arts of the South Pacific. Jean Guiart. Thames & Hudson, London

Behind the Ranges. J.P. Sinclair. Melbourne University Press

The Book of Pidgin English. John Murphy. W.R. Smith & Patterson Pty, Ltd., Brisbane

The Coastwatchers. Eric Feldt. Halstead Press, Sydney

The High Valley. Kenneth E. Read. Charles Scribners Sons, New York

The Last Unknown. Gavin Souter. Angus & Robertson

Patrol Into Yesterday, My New Guinea Years. J. McCarthy. F.W. Cheshire Pty., Ltd., Melbourne

Plumes & Arrows, Inside New Guinea. Colin Simpson. Halstead Press, Sydney

72. *Many people* living in the Western District came from these islands in the mouth of the Fly River.

-75. *Crocodiles* raised
George Craig, a hun-
r turned conservation-
, grow as large as the
ghteen foot monster
low. The baby croc-
liles on the left may
ok charming, but are
tually aggressive and
ngerous. Above, the
es of a full-grown
ocodile. The home of
these reptiles is Daru
and.

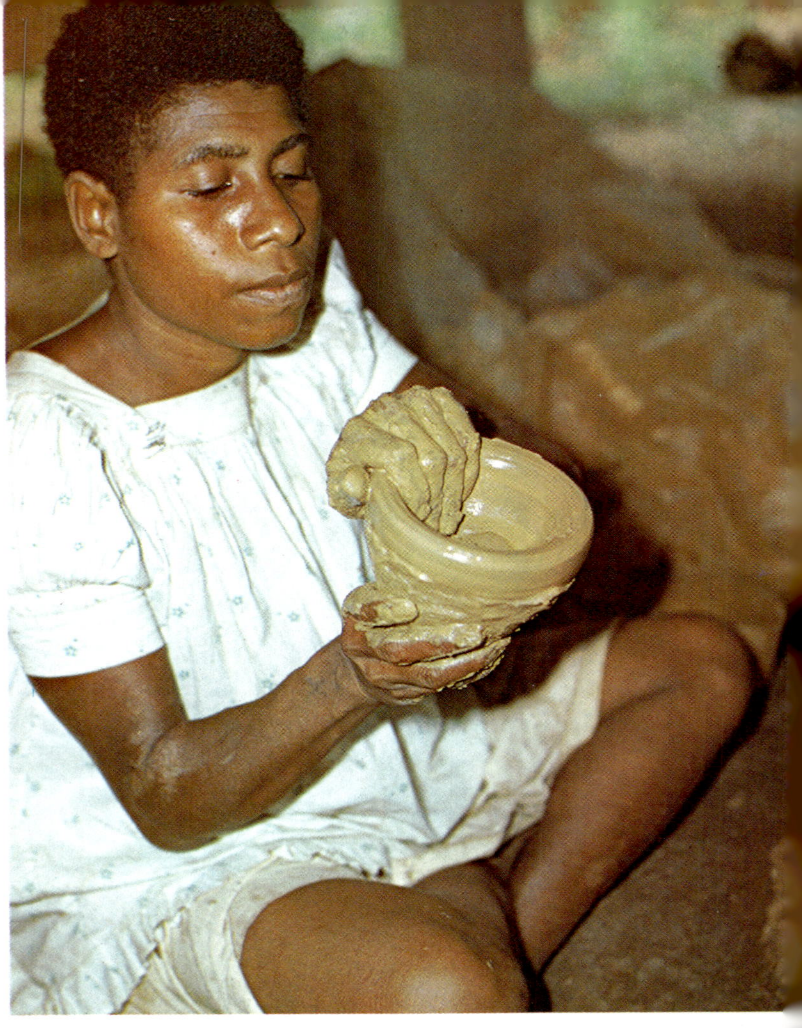

77. *Yabob people* from Madang District have decorated their pots with the same identification mark for centuries.

'6. *The potters* in Bilibil Village, ⁄ladang District, were taught the use ›f the potter's wheel by the United ⁄ations, but they still prefer their ›ld hand methods.

78. *Children* often carry bush knives to school and use them between classes to trim the nearby grass to reduce mosquito breeding grounds.

79. *A tattooed nursing sister* from Alexishafen Hospital, one of New Guinea's better medical facilities.

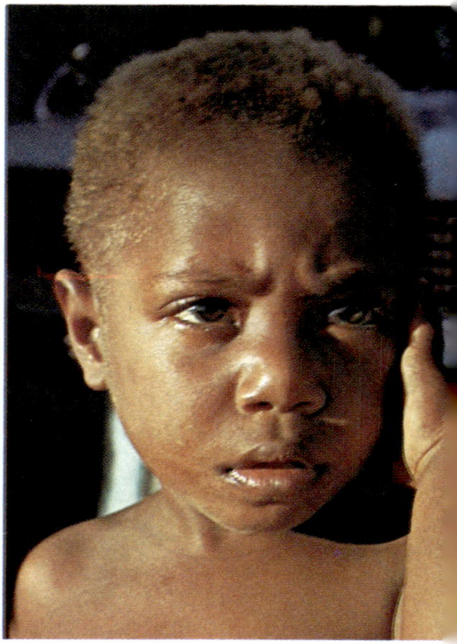

81. *Village Sunday schools* draw large crowds to participate in the singing and games.

80. *A small Tolai boy* from Rabaul, New Britain.

82. *The red hatband* signifies that this gentleman has been chosen to be a *tultul*, or government appointed native official. Christmas tinsel enjoys great popularity as a personal adornment.

83. *Portrait* of a man from Bougainville Island.

4. *Mount Bagana* is an active volcano on Bougainville. Its long smoke trail can be seen from many miles away.

86. *Sweet potatoes* provide the most ▶ important food in the diet of the majority of New Guinea's people.

85. *The Bougainville copper mine* is located near Kieta in a rugged, mountainous area. Passengers on incoming flights may get a view of the entire operation, if they are lucky enough to find a break in the clouds.

87. *Market vendors* in Rabaul weave their own bags from coconut palm leaves, since paper bags are too expensive.

38. *The wheely-wheely* is a favorite toy of children throughout New Guinea. It consists of a rolling disk of any available material fastened to the end of a stick.

39. *Betel nut* and peanut vendor in the public market of Rabaul.

90. *The Japanese* hid many small vessels in caves surrounding Rabaul Harbor to prevent their discovery by the Allies.

91. *Wrecks* of many Japanese aircraft can be found in the bush surrounding Rabaul airport. ▶

The walls of an un-
ground cave in the
ter of Rabaul are
ered with Japanese
tary charts and maps
n World War II.

93. *Landing barges* from World War II are still used by the government to haul heavy equipment.